T0123220

An Analysis of

Lucien Febvre's

The Problem of Unbelief in the 16th Century

Joseph Tendler

Published by Macat International Ltd
24:13 Coda Centre, 189 Munster Road, London SW6 6AW.

Distributed exclusively by Routledge
2 Park Square, Milton Park, Abingdon, Oxon OX14 4RN
711 Third Avenue, New York, NY 10017, USA

Routledge is an imprint of the Taylor & Francis Group, an informa business

www.macat.com
info@macat.com

Cataloguing in Publication Data
A catalogue record for this book is available from the British Library.
Library of Congress Cataloguing-in-Publication Data is available upon request.
Cover illustration: Etienne Gilfillan

ISBN 978-1-912302-53-6 (hardback)
ISBN 978-1-912128-85-3 (paperback)
ISBN 978-1-912281-41-1 (e-book)

Notice
The information in this book is designed to orientate readers of the work under analysis,
to elucidate and contextualise its key ideas and themes, and to aid in the development
of critical thinking skills. It is not meant to be used, nor should it be used, as a
substitute for original thinking or in place of original writing or research. References and
notes are provided for informational purposes and their presence does not constitute
endorsement of the information or opinions therein. This book is presented solely for
educational purposes. It is sold on the understanding that the publisher is not engaged
to provide any scholarly advice. The publisher has made every effort to ensure that
this book is accurate and up-to-date, but makes no warranties or representations with
regard to the completeness or reliability of the information it contains. The information
and the opinions provided herein are not guaranteed or warranted to produce particular
results and may not be suitable for students of every ability. The publisher shall not be
liable for any loss, damage or disruption arising from any errors or omissions, or from
the use of this book, including, but not limited to, special, incidental, consequential or
other damages caused, or alleged to have been caused, directly or indirectly, by the
information contained within.

CONTENTS

THE MACAT LIBRARY

The Macat Library is a series of unique academic explorations of seminal works in the humanities and social sciences – books and papers that have had a significant and widely recognised impact on their disciplines. It has been created to serve as much more than just a summary of what lies between the covers of a great book. It illuminates and explores the influences on, ideas of, and impact of that book. Our goal is to offer a learning resource that encourages critical thinking and fosters a better, deeper understanding of important ideas.

Each publication is divided into three Sections: Influences, Ideas, and Impact. Each Section has four Modules. These explore every important facet of the work, and the responses to it.

This Section-Module structure makes a Macat Library book easy to use, but it has another important feature. Because each Macat book is written to the same format, it is possible (and encouraged!) to cross-reference multiple Macat books along the same lines of inquiry or research. This allows the reader to open up interesting interdisciplinary pathways.

To further aid your reading, lists of glossary terms and people mentioned are included at the end of this book (these are indicated by an asterisk [*] throughout) – as well as a list of works cited.

Macat has worked with the University of Cambridge to identify the elements of critical thinking and understand the ways in which six different skills combine to enable effective thinking.
Three allow us to fully understand a problem; three more give us the tools to solve it. Together, these six skills make up the **PACIER** model of critical thinking. They are:

ANALYSIS – understanding how an argument is built
EVALUATION – exploring the strengths and weaknesses of an argument
INTERPRETATION – understanding issues of meaning

CREATIVE THINKING – coming up with new ideas and fresh connections
PROBLEM-SOLVING – producing strong solutions
REASONING – creating strong arguments

To find out more, visit **WWW.MACAT.COM.**

CRITICAL THINKING AND *THE PROBLEM OF UNBELIEF*

Primary critical thinking skill: INTERPRETATION
Secondary critical thinking skill: CREATIVE THINKING

Febvre asked this core question in *The Problem of Unbelief:* 'Could sixteenth-century people hold religious views that were not those of official, Church-sanctioned Christianity, or could they simply not believe at all?' The answer informed a wider debate on history, and particularly modern French history. Did the religious attitudes of the Enlightenment and the twentieth century—notably secularism and atheism—first take root in the sixteenth century? Could the spirit of scientific and rational inquiry have begun with the rejection of God and Christianity by men such as François Rabelais, writing in his allegorical novel *Gargantua and Pantagruel* – the work most often cited as a proto-"atheist" text prior to Febvre's study? The debate hinged on some key differences of interpretation. Was Rabelais mocking the structures of the Christian Church (in which case he might be anticlerical)? Was he mocking the Bible scriptures or Church doctrines (in which case he might be anti-Christian)? Or was he mocking the very idea of God's existence (in which case he might be an atheist)?

The other great contribution that Febvre made to the study of history can be found not so much in the fine detail of this work as in the additions that he made to the historian's toolkit. In this sense, Febvre was highly creative; indeed it can be argued that he ranks among the most creative of all historians. He sought to move the study of history itself beyond its traditional focus on documentary records, arguing instead that close analysis of language could open up a gateway into the ways in which people actually thought, and to their subconscious minds. This concept, the focus on "mentalities," is core to the hugely influential approach of the Annales group of historians, and it enabled a switch in the focus of much historical inquiry, away from the study of elites and their deeds and towards new forms of broader social history. Febvre also used techniques and models drawn from anthropology and sociology to create new ways of framing and answering questions, further extending the range of problems that could be addressed by historians. Working together with colleagues such as Marc Bloch, his understanding of what constituted evidence and of the meanings that could be attributed to it, radically redefined what history is – and what it should aspire to be.

ABOUT THE AUTHOR OF THE ORIGINAL WORK

Born in 1878 in Nancy, France, **Lucien Febvre** became one of his country's most important historians, writing numerous influential books and working with the French government to promote the subject he loved. He acted as an editor for the country's national encyclopedia, while also establishing new historical research centers. Remembered as a founder of the famous Annales school of history, Febvre pushed historians to look for clues in other disciplines and to focus on ordinary people's lives. He died in 1956.

ABOUT THE AUTHOR OF THE ANALYSIS

Dr Joseph Tendler received his PhD from the University of St Andrews. He is the author of *Opponents of the Annales School* (Palgrave, 2013).

ABOUT MACAT

GREAT WORKS FOR CRITICAL THINKING

Macat is focused on making the ideas of the world's great thinkers accessible and comprehensible to everybody, everywhere, in ways that promote the development of enhanced critical thinking skills.

It works with leading academics from the world's top universities to produce new analyses that focus on the ideas and the impact of the most influential works ever written across a wide variety of academic disciplines. Each of the works that sit at the heart of its growing library is an enduring example of great thinking. But by setting them in context – and looking at the influences that shaped their authors, as well as the responses they provoked – Macat encourages readers to look at these classics and game-changers with fresh eyes. Readers learn to think, engage and challenge their ideas, rather than simply accepting them.

'Macat offers an amazing first-of-its-kind tool for interdisciplinary learning and research. Its focus on works that transformed their disciplines and its rigorous approach, drawing on the world's leading experts and educational institutions, opens up a world-class education to anyone.'

Andreas Schleicher
Director for Education and Skills, Organisation for Economic Co-operation and Development

'Macat is taking on some of the major challenges in university education ... They have drawn together a strong team of active academics who are producing teaching materials that are novel in the breadth of their approach.'

Prof Lord Broers,
former Vice-Chancellor of the University of Cambridge

'The Macat vision is exceptionally exciting. It focuses upon new modes of learning which analyse and explain seminal texts which have profoundly influenced world thinking and so social and economic development. It promotes the kind of critical thinking which is essential for any society and economy.
This is the learning of the future.'

Rt Hon Charles Clarke, former UK Secretary of State for Education

'The Macat analyses provide immediate access to the critical conversation surrounding the books that have shaped their respective discipline, which will make them an invaluable resource to all of those, students and teachers, working in the field.'

Professor William Tronzo, University of California at San Diego

WAYS IN TO THE TEXT

KEY POINTS

- Lucien Febvre (1878–1956) was one of the most influential French thinkers of the twentieth century. He helped to pioneer important advances in historical method*—the way historians study the past.

- *The Problem of Unbelief* argues that atheism*—the refusal to believe in the existence of God—did not exist in the sixteenth century. This went against the commonly held views of historians.

- Febvre's problem-based* method—studying a particular aspect of the past and relating it to the present—changed how historians write history.

Who Was Lucien Febvre?

Born in 1878, Lucien Febvre grew up in Nancy, France. His father taught languages, and Febvre read many history books written in French, German, and English in his youth. Later, Febvre's career as a historian made him famous in France, as well as internationally.

In 1933, he was named professor at the Collège de France, an elite research institution where scholars gave only occasional lectures to the public. Febvre had plenty of time to write books and work with the French government to promote history. This included acting as an editor for the national encyclopedia, the *Encyclopédie française*, and helping establish new centers for research in history and the social sciences, such as the École des Hautes Études en Sciences Sociales (EHESS), which opened in Paris in 1947.

Febvre also played a key role in founding the *Annales* school,* which changed the way historians write history, pushing them to use interdisciplinary methods and to focus on ordinary people's lives in a way they had not done before. In 1929, Febvre and medieval historian Marc Bloch* cofounded a history periodical—*Annales d'Histoire Économique et Sociale*—in order to publish their ideas, and they developed a new, controversial approach to the study of history. This approach continues to influence how historians work today, encouraging them to examine the social, economic, and cultural lives of regular people.

What Does *The Problem of Unbelief* Say?

Lucien Febvre's book, *The Problem of Unbelief,* caused something of a sensation when it was published in France in 1942. It undermined a widely held view put forward by such French historians as Abel Lefranc,* Henri Busson,* Robert Lenoble,* and René Pintard.* They believed that the great sixteenth-century French writer François Rabelais* expressed views in his novel *Gargantua and Pantagruel* that made it plain he was extremely skeptical about Christianity as a whole. These historians felt that Rabelais was hiding behind a thin veneer of Christian faith and that he was, in fact, one of the first atheists. It was Rabelais and the barely concealed atheism he showed in his work that would later allow atheism and secularism—the separation of government institutions from the Church—to develop in modern France. Febvre argued against this view. He believed sixteenth-century writers' opinions on religion and God differed completely from those of modern writers. Febvre concluded that atheism did not—in fact *could not*—have existed in the sixteenth century. This conclusion is significant today as historians are still debating how old the concept of atheism is.

The book is also important because Febvre drew on several new ideas about the best ways to study history when he was writing it. These ideas helped to shape his work and have proved influential because they changed how later generations of historians thought as well. In this respect, *The Problem of Unbelief* can be seen as a key work for anyone interested in historiography,* the study of how history is written.

First, Febvre insisted that historians should begin their investigations by asking a question. In this case: "Did Rabelais hold un-Christian views?" His method required historians to tailor their approach specifically to the topics they studied. Febvre was the first historian to champion "problem-based" history, a method of studying a particular aspect of the past in detail and explaining its *relationship* to the present. "Problem" history moves away from the study of preset periods, such as the medieval or early-modern period, to focus on specific times and places in detail. This is a very different approach from the more traditional version, where all the possible facts were simply amassed and a story about past periods was then narrated. Historians have now embraced this key idea, and it is hard to remember that history was once written in any other way.

Second, Febvre championed the study of what are known as "mentalities."* Broadly this refers to mind-sets—distinct, shared ways of looking at the world and reacting to it. Febvre used this technique to do more than simply compare what Rabelais had written with Christian teachings. He actually studied the beliefs of groups of French people in the sixteenth century. It was this research that convinced him that Rabelais's ideas were not as unusual as other historians had thought.

Why Does *The Problem of Unbelief* Matter?

Febvre's book gives the reader three things. The first is a lesson in how to write history. The second is an evaluation of the problems posed in writing history. And the third is a view of Rabelais and sixteenth-century religious attitudes that remains current, if controversial, today. In this last respect, while such modern scholars as Jean-Pierre Cavaillé* and Alain Boureau* sometimes criticize Febvre, they also accept the findings of *The Problem of Unbelief* as extremely stimulating. Historians celebrate the book and refer to it today, but they also overlook elements of Febvre's work that make it ripe for reconsideration, such as his argument that a shift from an early-modern to a modern worldview happened in the seventeenth century, as well as its focus on how best to research and write history.

The questions Febvre studied in *The Problem of Unbelief* are fundamental for any historian. He wanted to understand what the past is and what we can know about it. He also sought to avoid introducing anachronism* into his writing—that is, assuming attitudes and using ideas that did not exist until much later. Febvre also tried to show that there were wide-ranging connections between what he was studying and other areas of history. His innovative way of thinking about and writing on the subject of history also makes *The Problem of Unbelief* a worthwhile topic for students in other areas, such as literary studies.

Understanding the past on its own terms and avoiding anachronism remains key to producing good work in history. But understanding the past on its own terms also relies on problem-solving methods used in the humanities and social sciences more generally—looking at people and ideas in context. The challenge of understanding the past requires researchers to tailor their approach to the subject. Using a variety of methods allows historians to explain events in terms of a number of different causes and factors.

SECTION 1
INFLUENCES

MODULE 1
THE AUTHOR AND THE HISTORICAL CONTEXT

KEY POINTS

- *The Problem of Unbelief* is written in a lively style that helps readers better understand ideas about sixteenth-century history, atheism,* and Rabelais* himself.

- World War I* changed Febvre's mind about how important the past is in shaping the present.

- *The Problem of Unbelief* was written in the 1930s, when the identity of both France and Europe was changing rapidly.

Why Read This Text?

Lucien Febvre's *The Problem of Unbelief* is a perfect example of a work of historical research that uses the mentalities* method to reach its conclusions. This method involves looking at the subconscious ideas and concepts through which people of any particular time view the world around them.

Febvre's lively and conversational writing style made this approach accessible to a wide audience, and readers can enjoy it either for what it reveals about sixteenth-century history, atheism, and Rabelais himself, or to learn from its arguments about how historians write history.

The Problem of Unbelief also remains central to understanding the *Annales* school. Since this school of historical thought and Febvre's methods underpin the professional practice of history today, no reader of history can ignore this book.[1] It introduces

> ❝ It is ironic that Lucien Febvre, a modern historian who worked with Marc Bloch to foster international exchange through the writing of problem-orientated histories of the whole range of human experiences, is relatively unknown beyond the mental frontiers of France. ❞
>
> Marnie Hughes-Warrington, *Fifty Key Thinkers on History*

them to—and then develops—basic concepts of historical analysis that are fundamental to the historian's craft, such as anachronism* and problem history.* Anachronism is an error whereby an idea, item, person, or phrase appears in a period to which it does not belong. Problem history is an approach to historical research that Febvre helped to develop. It identifies unexplained aspects of the present and provides a historical explanation of their origins using an interdisciplinary method.

The book has also encouraged research in the field of early-modern European religious beliefs, and that research continues across Europe and America today. Its use of the mentalities method and its study of popular beliefs of the time have raised the profile of ordinary people's lives and views, giving a voice to those previously ignored by historians. *The Problem of Unbelief* offers a varied reappraisal of history from new perspectives that are still being explored today.[2]

Author's Life
Febvre was born in 1878 in Nancy, eastern France. Throughout his life he retained a love of the area. His father studied and taught languages, and Lucien quickly found himself devouring works by authors writing in French, German, and English.[3]

Clearly a gifted student, at the age of 20 Febvre attended the respected École Normale Supérieure in Paris, where he studied history and geography. After graduating, he spent the four years between 1903 and 1907 at the Fondation Thiers, a research institute that sponsored young scholars working on their doctorates. He then moved into teaching while completing his thesis.

Febvre's career was put on hold in 1914 when World War I broke out, and he served in the French army for the four years of the conflict. He managed to return to academia in 1919, when he took up a post at the prestigious University of Strasbourg, where he remained for 14 years. During this time he met fellow historian Marc Bloch.* The two men shared many of the same views and would work together to develop a new approach to the study of history. This became known as the *Annales* school.[4]

In 1933 Febvre took up a senior position as chair for modern civilization at the prestigious Collège de France in Paris, and also worked on *The Problem of Unbelief*, which was published in 1937. He fell in with a circle of socialist professors, including Charles Andler,* Victor Basch,* and François Simiand.*[5] This group was committed to studying previously unrepresented social groups and attitudes, making use of the new social science disciplines such as anthropology (the study of human beings and culture) and sociology (the study of society) that were emerging at the time. Febvre was also interested in the relationship between the Renaissance* and modern France. The Renaissance was a long period of development in Europe between the fourteenth and seventeenth centuries that scholars believed had formed France's modern identity. As a young man, Febvre saw this as a very important time in French history, because it was this period (particularly from the sixteenth century onward) that had encouraged the kind of open-minded inquiries that had forged France's national identity. World War I changed Febvre's mind.[6] After the war, he came to believe that the pre-modern France of Rabelais was clearly different from Febvre's twentieth-century France. Indeed, he decided that it was dangerous to look for the seeds of the modern worldview in the distant past.[7]

Author's Background

Febvre wrote *The Problem of Unbelief* in 1930s France, when arguments over the best way to run the country dominated cultural and political life and France's identity was changing rapidly.[8] These disputes centered on the conflict between communism* and Nazism.* Communism emphasized the need for state ownership of all aspects of national infrastructure, such as the roads, railways, and air travel. Communists dreamed of ending capitalism, an economic system based on private ownership, private enterprise, and the maximization of profit. They wanted to abolish private property and create a new society based on justice and equality for all. Nazism, in contrast, stood for a radical new society based on racial superiority and the advancement of the nation state. A Nazi government ruled France's near neighbor, Germany, while a communist government was in place in the USSR,* which was France's ally at the time.

Febvre was more in favor of republicanism,* a form of government characterized by the active role of citizens and where the head of the government is selected not by rules of heredity but by other means, most commonly through elections. After the French Revolution* of 1789, France had experimented with a republican regime, which eventually became the lasting form of French government after 1871.[9] Febvre was a supporter of the values promoted by republican France: a secular* (or non-religious) state, rational thought on logical lines, equality of citizens before the law, and the values of universalism (the idea that France's culture was open to everybody). *The Problem of Unbelief* is about the very origins of the principles Febvre held dear, particularly the idea that France was a secular state. However, this was not simply abstract thinking.

The struggle to pass a law in 1905 that legally separated Church and state in France was still at the forefront of people's minds, even in the 1930s when Febvre was writing his book.[10]

NOTES

1   Joseph Tendler, "Variations on Realism, Method and Time: The *Annales* School," in *The Sage Handbook of Historical Theory*, ed. Nancy Partner and Sarah Foot (London: Sage, 2013), 67.

2   Tendler, "Variations on Realism, Method and Time," 67.

3   Bertrand Müller, *Lucien Febvre: Lecteur et critique* (Lucien Febvre: Reader and critic) (Paris: Albin Michel, 1994), 103.

4   Charles-Olivier Carbonell and Georges Livet, eds., *Au Berceau des Annales: Le milieu Strasbourgeois, l'histoire en France au début du XXe siècle* (At the crib of the *Annales*: The Strasbourg milieu, history in France at the beginning of the twentieth century) (Toulouse: Presses de l'Institut d'Études Politiques de Toulouse, 1979), xxiv.

5   Müller, *Lucien Febvre*, 110.

6   Eugen Weber, *The Hollow Years: France in the 1930s* (New York: Norton, 1996), 26–8.

7   Jonathon Dewald, *Lost Worlds: The Emergence of French Social History 1815–1970* (Pennsylvania, PA: Pennsylvania State University Press, 2006), 101–2.

8   Peter Schöttler, «Le Rhin comme enjeu historiographique dans l'entre-deux-guerres. Vers une histoire des mentalités frontalières" (The Rhine as a historiographical stake in the inter-war period. Toward a history of frontier mentalities), *Genèses* 14 (1994): 63–82.

9   Rod Kedward, *La Vie en bleu: France and the French since 1900* (London: Allen Lane, 2005), 186.

10 Isabel Noronha-DiVanna, *Writing History in the Third Republic* (Newcastle upon Tyne: Cambridge Scholars Publishing, 2010), 32, 41.

ACADEMIC CONTEXT

KEY POINTS

- The history of ideas* charts the evolution of ideas, showing how their meanings change over time.
- The history of popular religious beliefs remained underdeveloped and ignored in the first half of the twentieth century.
- Febvre developed the history of ideas by collaborating with scholars in other disciplines, such as anthropology, psychology, and sociology.

The Work in its Context

American and European historians developed the history of ideas—presenting the changes in human ideas and the way they're presented over time— throughout the early twentieth century, and particularly in the 1930s. Historians wanted to challenge existing understandings of history based on politics, religion, and military history. These historians investigated how ideas had altered their meanings over time as a result of widespread cultural and intellectual changes in societies at large. The fact that the lower social orders had not previously been a part of these political, religious, and military readings of history concerned them greatly.

American historian Arthur O. Lovejoy* was one of the best-known historians of ideas. His 1936 book, *The Great Chain of Being*, explored a notion from ancient Greek philosophy that a life force exists that originates with God. The life force then descends to Earth in a number of ways, including via angels, stars, the moon, kings and queens, and animals.[1] Lovejoy explored how writers and poets had always used this idea in literature to affect readers' thoughts

> **❝** The notion of mentalities as Febvre imagines it, which is intent on maintaining a bridge between psychology and sociology in the difficult debate that puts them on opposite sides of the question of individual consciousness and the collective unconscious, means to preserve the individual aspect and the place of psychology. **❞**
>
> André Burgière, *The Annales School: An Intellectual History*

and feelings. The book became an international best seller because it addressed a variety of disciplines—history, literature, philosophy, psychology, and theology—and so could reach a wide audience.

Overview of the Field

Lucien Febvre's attempt to write a history of popular beliefs in *The Problem of Unbelief* was an unusual break from the approach normally taken by other historians. As the discipline of history developed in the nineteenth century, what is known as scientific history mainly focused on manuscripts and other works kept in archives. People thought a historian's job was to collect and comment on documents that could be proved to be genuine—it was not to speculate about what might have been. The historian Gabriel Monod,* who had encouraged these scientific methods in France, thought historians should scrutinize documents as closely as philologists—people who study literature and language—did. Because the archives of documents had mainly been collected by governments, the histories they contained were largely concerned with what kings, ministers, clerics, and states had done.

There were, however, some early and influential exceptions in France. During the eighteenth century, the French thinker Voltaire* had called for historians not simply to uncover reliable facts about the past, but to pay attention to "customs, laws, mores, commerce, finance, agriculture, and population."[2] By "mores" Voltaire was referring to people's tastes—whether in literature, table linen, or art—suggesting that historians should study all facets of a society or civilization. In the nineteenth century, historian Jules Michelet* continued this trend by trying to reconstruct the lives of past communities. In the 1840s, Michelet lectured at France's most famous university, the Sorbonne, on the importance of rural peasants and industrial workers in shaping France's history. The results of these lectures appeared in his 1846 work, *Le Peuple* (The people), which called on historians to address the hopes and sufferings of the lower classes in French society.[3]

Academic Influences

Febvre wrote *The Problem of Unbelief* in the same tradition established by Voltaire and Michelet in France, but he combined it with twentieth-century developments led by Henri Berr* and Lucien Lévy-Bruhl.* Berr was Febvre's mentor; he too had restated the need to study ideas in historical perspective. Berr insisted that people could understand reality only by charting how all sorts of human ideas had evolved to understand the world.[4] Furthermore, he maintained that scholars must cooperate to study the evolution of all ideas, understanding each in its proper context. In this way scholars would eventually gain an overview of all human knowledge—what Berr termed a "synthesis."[5]

Lévy-Bruhl, meanwhile, wanted history to draw on the insights of other emerging social sciences, such as psychology and sociology. He asserted that simple social groups, whether peasants, workers, or exotic tribespeople, behaved in accordance with a mentality* (*mentalité*). His study of what he termed "primitive people" aimed to reveal "the orientation peculiar to this type of mind, what data it has at its command, how it acquires them, and what use it makes of them—in short, what the limits and contents of its experience are."[6]

By the early twentieth century, historians were encouraged to study not just single ideas but collective mental frameworks.

Just as Berr had encouraged people to do, Febvre draws on all this to emphasize the importance of redrawing a complete picture of sixteenth-century religious ideas: "Let us delight in what we were missing: a complete picture, and not just an outline, of the animated existence of the father of *Pantagruel* [i.e. Rabelais]."[7] Febvre also takes great care to look at individual mores (or tastes), just as Voltaire would have: "Let us now knock at the door of the theologians and controversialists … They each had different temperaments and different habits, and we have to take different precautions if we want to understand them and assess their testimony properly."[8] In other words, Febvre wants to look at the work of Rabelais's contemporaries as he tries to get a deeper understanding of the context in which Rabelais himself was working.

Febvre was exposed to these ideas after working with Berr—this much is clear by looking at what he published before *The Problem of Unbelief.* Articles summarizing Febvre's early research on Rabelais appeared in a journal edited by Berr himself, the *Revue de Synthèse* (Synthesis Review).[9] In these articles, Febvre dismantled the ideas built by twentieth-century historians around Rabelais. Two of the most important were that Rabelais was the father of modern atheism* and that his work meant ordinary people looked on the Church less favorably. He then gave a snapshot of how Rabelais's work did in fact demonstrate the nature of popular religious beliefs if it was investigated using an interdisciplinary method. By this, Febvre meant one that brought together the methods and concepts of all the humanities and social sciences to understand the past more fully. For example, using literary criticism to analyze texts or borrowing from anthropology to investigate social relations in past societies. This reversed errors previous historians had made by studying only fragments of the past.[10]

NOTES

1 Arthur O. Lovejoy, *The Great Chain of Being* (Cambridge, MA: Harvard University Press, 1936), 59.

2 See: Robert Darnton, *L'Aventure de l'Encyclopédie* (Cambridge: Cambridge University Press, 1979), ix.

3 Jules Michelet, *Le Peuple: Nos fils* (The people: Our sons) (Paris: Flammarion, 1846), 29.

4 Henri Berr, *La Synthèse en histoire* (Synthesis in history) (Paris: Albin Michel, 1911), 308.

5 Berr, *Synthèse en histoire*, i–vi.

6 Lucien Lévy-Bruhl, *La Mentalité primitive* (The primitive mentality) (Paris: PUF, 1922), 11.

7 Lucien Febvre, "L'Homme, la légende et l'œuvre. Sur Rabelais: Ignorances fondamentales" (The man, the legend, the work. On Rabelais: Fundamental ignorance), *Revue de Synthèse* 1 (1931): 1–31, 2.

8 Lucien Febvre, *The Problem of Unbelief in the Sixteenth Century: The Religion of Rabelais*, trans. Beatrice Gottlieb (Cambridge, MA: Harvard University Press, 1982), 101.

9 Febvre, "L'Homme, la légende et l'œuvre."

10 Febvre, "L'Homme, la légende et l'œuvre," 5–6.

THE PROBLEM

KEY POINTS

- Febvre and other scholars were trying to decide whether ordinary people and writers could actually dissent from (disagree with) Church teachings in the sixteenth century.

- Previously, Abel Lefranc* and others argued that the sixteenth century marked the start of a tradition of un-Christian thought in France, leading directly to modern atheism* and secularism.*

- Febvre reacts directly to this debate, using evidence from Rabelais* and his contemporaries' works to conclude that atheism was not possible at this time.

Core Question

Lucien Febvre asked this core question in *The Problem of Unbelief*: "Could sixteenth-century people hold religious views that were not those of official, Church-sanctioned Christianity, or could they simply not believe at all?" The answer informed a wider debate on modern history, particularly modern French history. Did the religious attitudes of the Enlightenment* and the twentieth century—notably secularism and atheism—first take root in the sixteenth century? Could the spirit of scientific and rational* inquiry of the twentieth century have begun with the rejection of God and Christianity by men such as Rabelais?[1] The debate hinged on some key differences of interpretation. Was Rabelais mocking the structures of the Christian Church (in which case he might be anticlerical)? Was he mocking the Bible scriptures or Church doctrines (in which case he might be anti-Christian)? Or was he

> ❝ To believe or not to believe. The naive, simplistic notion that the problem is without mystery, the anti-historical notion that we can deal with it with regard to the men of the sixteenth century in the same way we tend to deal with it with regard to ourselves—this illusion and these anachronisms are what this whole book has been directed against. ❞
>
> Lucien Febvre, *The Problem of Unbelief*

mocking the very idea of God's existence (in which case he might be an atheist)?

This wider debate reveals the second, less obvious, core question concealed in questions about atheism. How should historians properly investigate past ideas to understand what people really believed at that time? Febvre wrote in *The Problem of Unbelief* that "It is … a search for a method, or, to be more precise, a critical examination of a complex of problems—historical, psychological, and methodological."[2] However, it was one thing for historians to understand a particular belief held by an actor in the past. It was quite another to try to capture an idea of non-belief or unbelief.

The Participants

A number of historians and literary critics directed their attention to these core questions. An older generation of scholars—notable figures such as Henri Busson,* Robert Lenoble,* René Pintard,* and Abel Lefranc*—did so just before the period in which Febvre worked. All of them studied anti-Christian literature and philosophy in the sixteenth century. They saw it as allied to the growth of rationalism, the mental attitude that viewed science and experimentation as the key to finding out the truth about the world.

Busson, Lefranc, and Pintard argued that Rabelais attacked

Christianity. They saw his writings as a form of early atheism or anticlericalism that encouraged his readers to criticize Church leaders.[3] For these scholars, modern society emerged during the time of the Renaissance,* the time when Rabelais lived and worked. Because the ideas held in a modern society took root at this time, for these historians the sixteenth century resembled the twentieth century they knew—at least in that sense. Lenoble, meanwhile, worked on the history of science and also found that hostility to religion usually translated into hostility to the Church and to the government.[4]

Rabelais's *Gargantua and Pantagruel* was written as five different novels, roughly between 1532 and 1564. The titles of the five books, in the order they were published, are as follows:

- *Pantagruel*
- *Gargantua*
- *The Third Book of Pantagruel*
- *The Fourth Book of Pantagruel*
- *The Fifth Book of Pantagruel*

Abel Lefranc followed in the footsteps of the literary scholar Louis Thuasne,* and both men identified the imagery and hidden fragments of atheist and anti-Christian thought in *Pantagruel*.[5] However, none of these historians or critics suggested it was a clear-cut issue to understand where Rabelais stood on atheist or anti-Christian views. It was not. Each man nonetheless rejected the classic position—that Rabelais's work simply reflected its era.[6]

Lucien Febvre's studies of sixteenth-century religious practice placed him in a broader group of international scholars working on this topic. He relied at least to a certain degree on the work of English philosopher Bertrand Russell* and Sicilian philosopher Giovanni Gentile* with regard to his understanding of what sixteenth-century philosophy Rabelais would have read. Meanwhile,

American historian Lynn Thorndike's* work on sixteenth-century religion contributed to Febvre's understanding of humanist* thought. Humanist scholars in the sixteenth century wanted to revitalize Christian scholarship and the Christian Church by learning from ancient Greek and Roman scholars. This sometimes led to a strained relationship with the Church of the day.

The Contemporary Debate

The debate between Febvre and others remained subtle and nuanced, although its tone was somewhat controversial. While Febvre criticized the methods of the older generation of scholars working on anti-Christian beliefs, he did not see himself as proposing totally opposed arguments. Instead, Febvre attempted something more complicated than is obvious at first sight.

He agreed with Henri Busson that rationalism pervaded the modern world, a world in which scientific method clarified the nature of reality. Busson and others thought the call to rationalism came earlier than the famous French philosopher René Descartes,* writing in the seventeenth century. Busson dated it to 1533, when the French author Étienne Dolet* spoke out against Christianity in the southern French city of Toulouse.[7] Abel Lefranc put the date at 1532, the year that Rabelais's *Pantagruel* was published.[8] What was certain, though, was that the idea of rationalism had definitely appeared by the time of Descartes's death in 1650.

Yet what Febvre wanted to know was when this scientific rationalism evolved into an alternative—or even a hostile competitor—to Christianity in the same way that it had developed in the twentieth century. Busson and Lefranc saw its origins in Rabelais. Febvre did not. He accepted that unbelievers existed, but saw them as a minority without mainstream followers.[9] Febvre also argued that unbelievers could not reason rationally outside the framework of Christian belief structures at this point. So unbelievers could not gain atheist followers until *after* Descartes.[10] Like Busson and others, Febvre had studied the idea of unbelief. One of his major books on the topic, *Origène et Des Périers*, was published in 1942, the same year as *The Problem of Unbelief*.[11] In it, Febvre studied the unbelief of a writer called Bonaventure Des Périers,* a contemporary of Rabelais. Des Périers's work, like that of Rabelais, caused a scandal at the time because it seemed to go against Christian views. Febvre thought Des Périers did not believe in a Christian God.[12]

The difference between Febvre and Lefranc and Busson was that Febvre did not think secularism and atheism had their origins in Rabelais's work, because he believed it was not possible for people in the sixteenth century to think outside the bounds of Christianity. According to Febvre, the furthest anyone could go was to say that sixteenth-century people did not always believe in a Christian God while still thinking within the well-established frameworks of Christian beliefs. Therefore it was impossible to argue that active rejection of God—meaning atheism—existed at all.

NOTES

1   Lucien Febvre, *The Problem of Unbelief in the Sixteenth Century*, trans. Beatrice Gottlieb (Cambridge, MA: Harvard University Press, 1982), 460.

2   Febvre, *The Problem of Unbelief*, 8.

3   René Pintard, *Le Libertinage érudit* (Paris: Boivin, 1943), 5.

4   Robert Lenoble, *Mersenne, ou la naissance du mécanisme* (Paris: Vrin, 1943), 243.

5   Louis Thuasne, *Études sur Rabelais* (Studies of Rabelais) (Paris: Bouillon, 1904).

6   *Henri Hauser*, "De l'humanisme et de la Reforme en France," *Revue Historique* 64 (*1897*): 258–9.

7   Febvre, *The Problem of Unbelief*, 268.

8   Abel Lefranc, *Les Navigations de Pantagruel* (The seafaring of Pantagruel) (Paris: Leclerc, 1905), 15.

9   Lucien Febvre, "Dolet, Propagator of the Gospel" (1945), in *A New Kind of History*, Lucien Febvre, ed. Peter Burke (London: Harper & Row, 1973), 108–59.

10 Lucien Febvre, "Aux Origines de l'esprit moderne: Libertinisme, naturalisme, mécanisme" (On the origins of the modern spirit: Libertinism, naturalism, mechanism), in *Au Cœur religieux du XVIe siècle* (At the religious heart of the sixteenth century), Lucien Febvre (Paris: Editions EHESS, 1957), 337–58.

11 Lucien Febvre, *Origène et Des Périers, ou l'énigme du* Cymbalum Mundi (Paris: Droz, 1942).

12 Febvre, *Origène et Des Périers*, iii–x.

MODULE 4
THE AUTHOR'S CONTRIBUTION

KEY POINTS

- Febvre wanted to work out whether Rabelais* held un-Christian or atheist* views by understanding his words in the true context of his sixteenth-century times.

- Febvre overturned existing understandings of Rabelais— that he expressed an early atheism—by showing he did no such thing.

- *The Problem of Unbelief* challenged consensus views about Rabelais.

Author's Aims

Lucien Febvre, author of *The Problem of Unbelief,* read Rabelais and sought to understand his beliefs based on the context of the writer's times. His conclusion was that sixteenth-century men and women could not have held atheist views because of the general state of people's knowledge and the Christian framework at that time. Rather, Febvre believed that Rabelais pursued "the great dream of unifying the Christian world, of incorporating into a renewed Christianity peoples who until then had been strangers and enemies to Christianity."[1] Reformation* intellectuals prized this goal above all others. They aimed not to destroy the Church, as Abel Lefranc* implied, but to renew it, both in its teachings and the practices of the clergy.[2]

Febvre's response to the problem of Rabelais's religious views showed the flaws in preexisting historical scholarship. He highlighted in particular the problem of anachronism,* an error of chronology whereby an item, person, or phrase appears in a period in which it

> ❝ In 1942 Lucien Febvre published what has long been regarded as one of the masterpieces of Annales history in general, and the finest example of the *histoire des mentalités* in particular. ❞
>
> David Wootton, "Lucien Febvre and the Problem of Unbelief in the Early Modern Period," *Journal of Modern History*

does not belong. Febvre's forensic analysis of *what* was written by Rabelais, as well as by other writers, theologians, and scholars—and *when*—revealed that Lefranc projected his own views into the past. Lefranc assumed that science and Christianity were at odds, with one focused on belief, the other on reason and experiment. He then projected this tension back into the sixteenth century. Febvre said that for Rabelais, this tension did not exist. He warned: "Let us guard against projecting this modern conception of science onto the learning of our ancestors. It is an impossible fit."[3]

Approach

Febvre was able to look at the question of Rabelais's potential atheism by using the work of anthropologists (those who study human societies) and linguists (those who study the use of language). This offered a new way to tackle the question, because older scholars such as Abel Lefranc, Henri Busson,* and Robert Lenoble* approached it purely by reading and analyzing what Rabelais wrote. Popular beliefs—for example, that miracles occurred or that spirits protected people from misfortune—interested Febvre because they showed how history and psychology combined in anthropology.[4] Febvre was also drawn to sociology—a new discipline at the time. Sociology looked to study social relations in a scientific manner and had been pioneered in France by Émile Durkheim.*[5] Febvre's interest in language, meanwhile, fed into the study of mentality,* the investigation of the subconscious notions and concepts by which past peoples viewed the world around them.

French historians of the generation that taught Febvre specialized in the close scrutiny of documentary records about the past. Close analysis of Rabelais's language became a way to get to his inner thought processes. Febvre was constantly aware of the danger of presuming that authors represented their own true beliefs in the words of the characters they invented. Febvre asks, "Can a man be known from one work? Hasn't the author covered his face with a mask? Do the mask's features—coarse, exaggerated, caricatured—really represent the true face of the satirist?"[6]

Febvre also put his own twist on exactly these approaches, proceeding in *The Problem of Unbelief* in the manner of a judge who directs police and lawyers to the evidence they should collect. This role is known as an investigating magistrate in France. Febvre describes the procedure of examining evidence as "investigating a case, of weighing testimony—that of Rabelais's friends and enemies, that of Rabelais himself from the evidence of his life and works. This is a case we are about to reopen."[7] So Febvre was looking for a conclusive verdict. But he also wanted to explain the ideas of Rabelais's contemporaries and to show his readers what they thought. Febvre adopted the methods of historians from his teachers' generation—for example, Charles-Victor Langlois,* who said: "The best method to communicate to the public the most easily assimilated results of our work is not writing general histories, it is to present the documents themselves."[8]

Contribution in Context

The Problem of Unbelief developed first and foremost out of Febvre's interest in sixteenth-century religious history. This was a highly original area of study at the time.[9] His interest could be seen in an important early article he wrote on Protestantism.*[10] Here, Febvre described how members of the Church and related organizations reacted to new works of theology* and then conveyed their understanding of it to their congregations. This study of popular religion based on people's behavior came directly before *The Problem of Unbelief*.

The text was also original because of the challenge it posed to existing understandings of Rabelais—the idea that Rabelais held atheist views and did not believe in Christianity. Febvre took an entirely opposite stance. This new idea surfaced in the first half of the twentieth century during a period of sustained interest in Rabelais, created by the work of both Anatole France* and Abel Lefranc. The former had written a book arguing that it was Rabelais who had begun a long tradition in France of free thinking that ignored Church teachings.[11] Equally, in 1903, Lefranc had founded the Society for Rabelaisian Studies, which also had its own journal, known as the *Review for Rabelaisian Studies*. This organization promoted a method of studying texts as self-contained pieces of writing, which meant that if a reader wanted to truly know what a text said, the best way to find out was to study it closely and interpret it.[12] Febvre's contribution—using an interdisciplinary method to understand something more fully—took on a new school of literary criticism that centered on Lefranc's interpretations of Rabelais's work.

NOTES

1 Lucien Febvre, *The Problem of Unbelief in the Sixteenth Century*, trans. Beatrice Gottlieb (Cambridge, MA: Harvard University Press, 1982), 458.

2 Febvre, *The Problem of Unbelief*, 461.

3 Febvre, *The Problem of Unbelief*, 419.

4 Lucien Lévy-Bruhl, *La Mentalité primitive* (The primitive mentality) (Paris: PUF, 1922).

5 Émile Durkheim, *Les Règles de la méthode sociologique* (The rules of the sociological method) (Paris: Alcan, 1895), vii–viii, 5–19.

6 Febvre, *The Problem of Unbelief*, 153.

7   Febvre, *The Problem of Unbelief*, 16.

8   Charles-Victor Langlois, *La Vie en France au Moyen Âge d'après quelques moralistes du temps* (Life in medieval France according to some moralists of the period) (Paris: Hachette, 1908), ii.

9   Jacqueline Pluet-Despatin and Giles Candar, eds., *Lucien Febvre: Lettres à Henri Berr* (Paris: Fayard, 1997), 263.

10   Lucien Febvre, "Une Question mal posée: Les Origines de la Réforme française et le problème général des causes de la Réforme" (An ill-conceived question: The origins of the French Reformation and the general problem of the causes of the Reformation), *Revue Historique* 161 (1929): 1–73.

11   Abel Lefranc, *Les Navigations de Pantagruel* (The seafaring of Pantagruel) (Paris: Leclerc, 1905), 21–2; Anatole France, *Rabelais* (Paris: Calmann-Lévy, 1928), iv.

12   Natalie Zemon Davis, "Beyond Babel: Multiple Tongues and National Identities in Rabelais and his Critics," In *Confronting the Turkish Dogs: A Conversation on Rabelais and His Critics*, ed. Timothy Hampton (Berkeley: University of California Press, 1998), 15–28.

SECTION 2
IDEAS

MAIN IDEAS

KEY POINTS

- Febvre insisted that historians must integrate history and the social sciences.

- By understanding Rabelais's* "mental tools,"* Febvre believed he could reveal the writer's true religious views.

- Febvre's lively writing style makes *The Problem of Unbelief* engaging and enjoyable to read, but his constant allusions can make the meaning of some points unclear.

Key Themes

Lucien Febvre highlights three key themes—his aims for the development of historical study—throughout *The Problem of Unbelief*:

- The importance of analysis and synthesis to reach sound conclusions
- The need for historians to adopt an interdisciplinary approach
- The potential for history to qualify as a science when practiced properly.

Febvre wanted historians to collaborate with and borrow from methods used in anthropology, ethnology, and other social sciences to help achieve these goals. What particularly excited Febvre was the idea that history really could be a science. Like his friend Marc Bloch* and other members of the *Annales* school,* Febvre believed that if historians asked questions about the past and investigated them rigorously, then their work would resemble that of scientists,

> ❝ Like their contemporaries [the theologians],
> the poets, they were sixteenth-century men. They
> belonged to a century far-removed from our own,
> despite appearances—far removed most of all in its
> mental structure. ❞
>
> Lucien Febvre, *The Problem of Unbelief*

who formulated hypotheses (proposed explanations of phenomena) and then proved or disproved them using experiments. The idea of a history laboratory fascinated Febvre and Bloch in an era when scientific discoveries were really capturing people's imaginations.[1] This attachment to science accompanied a preference by historians of the *Annales* school for what was called "positive" knowledge. In other words, Febvre wanted to make it possible for historians to test the findings of other historians.[2] In having this aim, the *Annales* school drew inspiration from contemporary developments in social science methodologies developed by the sociologist Émile Durkheim* and those to which Febvre had been introduced through collaborations with his mentor Henri Berr.*

Exploring the Ideas

The idea of mentality and mental tools provided the framework for Febvre's argument that Rabelais did not hold atheist* or un-Christian ideas. Mentality in this context means the study of the subconscious notions and concepts by which past peoples view the world around them. Because people in all different ages exhibit a mentality, Febvre believed he could study social change by measuring how mentalities changed and evolved. Febvre could study Rabelais, but also look across societies and at intellectuals who were contemporaries of Rabelais, for example at the Dutch philosopher Erasmus* and the German theologian Martin Luther.*

As Febvre explained, "unbelief changes with the period. Sometimes it changes very rapidly—just as concepts change, those on which some people rely in order to make denials, while their neighbors use others in order to prop up the systems under attack."[3]

Mental tools fed into Febvre's idea of analysis and synthesis because they provided the critical social context against which he could assess whether Rabelais had held un-Christian views. Mental tools provided "the setting, conditions, and possibilities"—the synthesis, in other words—of ordinary people's views of the world. Looking at mentalities also provided an understanding of the Church's theological doctrine, which historians could study across space and over time.[4] Febvre even went so far as to state that the rediscovery and analysis of mentalities in any period "is what the historian's task really is."[5] Mentalities remained exclusive to the time and the place in which the people who used them were living.[6] Febvre insisted that a "civilization or an era has no assurance that it will be able to transmit these mental tools in their entirety to succeeding civilizations and eras."[7] He found that sixteenth-century mental tools did not resemble those of the twentieth century in any way at all. Sixteenth-century citizens had inherited the Christian belief of their forebears. But in the twentieth century, people had inherited atheistic views as well. Febvre's view on mentalities differed from what Abel Lefranc,* Henri Busson,* and others had found, so it required innovative use of the concept of mentality to be properly historicized.[8]

The Problem of Unbelief also proposed the idea that history could adopt the methods of laboratory science to produce certain results. All the members of the *Annales* school shared this main idea. Marc Bloch also believed that methods of analysis and synthesis produced scientific certainty. His book on the popular medieval belief that British and French kings had miraculous powers to heal deadly diseases also looked at the idea of mentalities.[9] Bloch described them as "psycho-social phenomena" necessitating the use of an "analytical method that by analysis extends to scientific synthesis."[10] The prestige of science and scientific discoveries in the early 1900s had fascinated Febvre and so encouraged his use of concepts such as mentality to try to make history scientific. It was in this period that the great physicist Albert Einstein* had formulated his theory of relativity* and in doing so transformed how scientists understood the material world. Febvre lived through this time and watched with interest.[11] He hoped that history could become the "science of man in time," showing people to what extent human beings had created a better life for themselves and what remained to be done.[12]

Language and Expression

Febvre expressed his argument elegantly. He modeled his energetic writing style on that of his doctoral supervisor, Gabriel Monod,* who himself was inspired by the dramatic writing of the famous French historian Jules Michelet.* Monod had written about Michelet and understood how important it was for history to be written in an engaging style. It had to bring to life the ways people in the past had thought about and understood their worlds—a combination of literary writing and psychological observation.[13] To that end, Febvre wrote *The Problem of Unbelief* in a "conversational" way, but with the energy and varied expression of an enthusiast on a mission to change readers' views about Rabelais.[14]

Even so, Febvre's writing can confuse readers. His habit of referring to many different books, ideas, and social movements may baffle those who do not know the sixteenth century as intimately as he does. For example, while discussing the resurrection of a central character (Epistemon) in Rabelais's *Pantagruel*, Febvre speculates, "Our investigation is in the light of reason alone."[15] This is not easy for a reader unfamiliar with the key ideas of European philosophy to understand. Why? Because here Febvre is referring to a tradition in German philosophy, Kantianism.*

NOTES

1   Bertrand Müller, ed., *Marc Bloch, Lucien Febvre et les Annales d'Histoire économique et sociale: Correspondance*, Bloch to Febvre, June 18, 1938 (Paris: Fayard, 1994–2003), 3:29.

2   Paul Ricoeur, *The Contribution of French Historiography to the Theory of History: The Zaharoff Lecture for 1978–1979* (Oxford: Clarendon Press, 1980), 21.

3   Lucien Febvre, *The Problem of Unbelief in the Sixteenth Century*, trans. Beatrice Gottlieb (Cambridge, MA: Harvard University Press, 1982), 460.

4   Febvre, *The Problem of Unbelief*, 171–2.

5   Febvre, *The Problem of Unbelief*, 355.

6   Febvre, *The Problem of Unbelief*, 355.

7   Febvre, *The Problem of Unbelief*, 150.

8   Febvre, *The Problem of Unbelief*, 464.

9   Marc Bloch, *The Royal Touch: Sacred Monarchy and Scrofula in England and France*, trans. J. E. Anderson (London, 1973; originally published in French in 1924), 243.

10 Marc Bloch, Méthodologie historique," unpublished notes.

11 Lucien Febvre, "Sur Einstein et sur l'histoire: Méditation de circonstance» (On Einstein and history: A meditation on circumstances), *Annales. Économies, Sociétés, Civilisations* 10 (1955): 305–12.

12 Lucien Febvre, "Vers une autre histoire" (Toward another history), *Revue de Métaphysique et de Morale* 63 (1949): 233, 229.

13 Gabriel Monod, *Renan, Taine, Michelet: Les Maîtres d'histoire* (Renan, Taine, Michelet: The masters of history) (Paris: Calmann-Lévy, 1894), 57.

14 Beatrice Gottlieb, introduction to Febvre, *The Problem of Unbelief*, xxxi.

15 Febvre, *The Problem of Unbelief*, 213.

"

SECONDARY IDEAS

KEY POINTS

- Three secondary themes run throughout the text. First, the epistemological* break of the seventeenth century, when scientific knowledge became more important than religious belief. Second, the nature of modern science. Third, the concept of time and the use of the senses in sixteenth-century cultural history.

- The secondary ideas add weight to Febvre's thesis that atheism* could not have existed in Rabelais's lifetime.

- The nature of modern science is the most important secondary idea because it informs both Febvre's conclusions about Rabelais and the problem history method* he uses.

Other Ideas

The Problem of Unbelief sets out four of Lucien Febvre's secondary ideas, which he put forward as part of his analysis of Rabelais's Christian beliefs. First, Febvre explored the idea that the European mentality* changed direction between 1500 and 1650, abandoning religion, mysticism, and God and instead looking to laboratory science and experimentation to understand the world. We can describe this fundamental change in European knowledge—or epistemology—as an "epistemological caesura." That is, a shift in how we know things from one set of thought processes to another.[1]

Developing this idea, Febvre carefully identified how twentieth-century laboratory and social sciences differed from sixteenth-century science. This was an important addition to one of the book's

> **❝** Is *[The Problem of Unbelief]* a monograph on a man, Rabelais? As great as he was, I would not have bothered to write that. It is rather, a search for a method, or, to be more precise, a critical examination of a complex of problems—historical, psychological, and methodological.**❞**
>
> Lucien Febvre, *The Problem of Unbelief*

main ideas—that of analysis and synthesis—because it helped to show how different the sixteenth century was from the twentieth century. In addition, Febvre also developed a related idea about how perceptions of time itself were different in the sixteenth century. Sixteenth-century men and women did not rely on clocks to understand time as we do today. Instead, they looked to natural events such as the rising and setting of the sun each day, or their recollection of how long the previous year felt. This pushed Febvre to think about the aspects in which the daily routine of sixteenth-century people did not give rise to, or resemble, twentieth-century ways of life. In doing so, Febvre reinforced the argument that Rabelais's ideas of Christian belief differed from twentieth-century ideas such as atheism on another level.

Exploring the Ideas

Febvre implies the epistemological shift in European mentality, rather than openly discussing it, throughout *The Problem of Unbelief*. This is important because scholars then as now have debated when the modern worldview as we know it actually began. Febvre accepts that at some point between the publication of Rabelais's *Pantagruel* in 1532 and the lifetime of the great French philosopher René Descartes* (1596–1650) it became possible to think both inside *and* outside Christian doctrine without offending traditional beliefs. However,

Febvre was adamant that "it is utter madness to make Rabelais the first name in a linear series at the tail end of which we put the 'free thinkers' of the twentieth century."[2] It is true, though, that Descartes and others certainly did experiment on the material world of minerals, animals, and cells and explain them in a new scientific language.

Febvre explored the differences between Descartes's science and modern science, carefully explaining how different the sixteenth-century version was from modern laboratory sciences. This meant he had to separate the meaning of "science" in the twentieth century from its meaning in the sixteenth century. He did not want "a 'clear' science that had not yet come into existence" to be confused with modern understandings of the term.[3] Science can now mean laboratory science conducted by scientists, or it can mean any organized body of knowledge in general. French, German, and Italian speakers will find the second meaning of science as "knowledge in general" natural, given that their languages preserve that meaning in current usage today. This meaning has all but disappeared in the Anglo-American world, however.[4] In the sixteenth century, "science" referred to any organized body of knowledge that became scientific based on the fact that it contained information organized by some principle. The fact that this meaning had disappeared by the twentieth century made it difficult for anyone but practitioners of laboratory science—usually biologists, chemists, and physicists—to claim that their findings had any "scientific" credibility or certainty.[5]

Febvre also argues that seeing something as related to time—for instance, three thirty or four o'clock—differs in the twentieth century from how it was perceived in the sixteenth century. Sixteenth-century clocks (when they existed at all) showed the hours only and were usually located solely in public places.[6] So Rabelais and his contemporaries had no more than a vague impression of time: "Fancifulness, imprecision, inexactness everywhere."[7] People relied more on their own personal experiences of time—of days passing—rather than clock measurements. Febvre shows that we too, even in the age of the watch and nuclear clock, make our personal history with our own memories. We do this by connecting events separated in time. For Febvre, we "make the past according to our dispositions." The big difference is that we now measure time much more precisely.[8]

Overlooked

Febvre's work in *The Problem of Unbelief* is now seen by scholars as key to understanding the ideas of the *Annales* school* and as characterizing early twentieth-century scholarship on religion and the modern world. Examples of other works of the era include German sociologist Max Weber's* *The Protestant Ethic and the Spirit of Capitalism*, which appeared in print in 1904 and was translated into English in 1930. Weber, like Febvre, also looked to the early-modern period to see if the origins of modern social, economic, and intellectual life existed there. He examined the interaction of religious belief and new rational* organizations of society. Febvre had been aware of Weber's work in his early years, but disagreed with his belief that the origins of modernity existed in the early-modern period.[9]

The Problem of Unbelief leaves questions about popular beliefs unanswered. The idea of an epistemological break that Febvre raised has not received any attention.[10] In addition, in his comments about our variable perception of time, Febvre thought that we each form our own past from our memories. If this is so, how might historians write works that others will understand? In this way, history would become deeply individual if any one historian were to write only from his or her own experiences. How historians write about the past—a collection of events in a time now passed—continues to perplex professional scholars, just as it did Febvre.[11]

NOTES

1   Jonathon Dewald, *Lost Worlds: The Emergence of French Social History 1815–1970* (Pennsylvania, PA: Pennsylvania State University Press, 2006), 101.

2   Lucien Febvre, *The Problem of Unbelief in the Sixteenth Century*, trans. Beatrice Gottlieb (Cambridge, MA: Harvard University Press, 1982), 460.

3   Febvre, *The Problem of Unbelief*, 423.

4   Fritz K. Ringer, *The Decline of the German Mandarins: The German Academic Community 1890–1933* (Cambridge, MA: Harvard University Press, 1990), 100–2.

5   Laurence R. Veysey, *The Emergence of the American University* (Chicago, IL: Chicago University Press, 1965), 127.

6   Febvre, *The Problem of Unbelief*, 394.

7   Febvre, *The Problem of Unbelief*, 395.

8   Febvre, *The Problem of Unbelief*, 398.

9   Bertrand Müller, *Lucien Febvre: Lecteur et critique* (Lucien Febvre: Reader and critic) (Paris: Albin Michel, 1994), 91.

10 David Wootton, "Lucien Febvre and the Problem of Unbelief in the Early Modern Period," *Journal of Modern History* 60 (1988): 721.

11 Joseph Tendler, "*Annales* Historians' Contested Transformations of Locality," in *Place and Locality in Modern France*, ed. Philip Whalen and Patrick Hutton (London: Bloomsbury, 2014), 59.

MODULE 7
ACHIEVEMENT

KEY POINTS

- *The Problem of Unbelief* is a fine example of how to research history and then write about it based on the history of ideas.*

- The rise of socioeconomic history in the interwar period led to a demand for Febvre's style of history and helped him become more respected.

- Febvre's methodology has been adopted by a number of historians, but predominantly in Europe and America rather than elsewhere in the world.

Assessing the Argument

Even today, scholars like to think about how successful Lucien Febvre was in demonstrating that Rabelais did not hold atheist* views. Historians including Georges Duby,* Jacques Le Goff,* and Natalie Zemon Davis* regard *The Problem of Unbelief* as an unrivaled example of how to research and write based on the history of ideas approach.[1]

Febvre used interdisciplinary concepts and a method inspired by both the history of ideas and the philosophy of history to find out the truth about Rabelais's religious attitudes. This framework of analysis was typical of the way in which Febvre approached the revision of historical interpretations he viewed as incorrect. Colleagues in the *Annales* school* saw the style used by Febvre in *The Problem of Unbelief*—including the feel of court proceedings and the inclusion of jokes—as amusing.[2] Others found it to be mocking in tone—more "black humor"—while yet others felt that "sentencing and encyclicals are part of [Febvre's] bequest" to later

> **❝** All in all, the deep religiosity of the majority of those who created the modern world, a phrase that applies to someone like Descartes, was, I hope I have shown, applicable a century earlier to Rabelais, and to those whose deep faith he knew how to express superbly. **❞**
>
> Lucien Febvre, *The Problem of Unbelief*

members of *Annales*.[3] In other words, Febvre's manner of delivering judgment on the work of other historians became a way of working adopted by later members of the *Annales* school.

Other landmark studies of Rabelais's relationship to popular beliefs did not revise Febvre's argument, and this highlights the respect he enjoyed among other scholars. As French philosopher Paul Ricoeur* pointed out, the world-renowned Russian literary theorist Mikhail Bakhtin* did not differ from Febvre in his "groundbreaking book" on Rabelais that appeared in the 1960s.[4] This shows that Febvre's achievements were generally acknowledged in the academic community.

Achievement in Context

The Problem of Unbelief first became widely accessible to English-speaking audiences in 1982, when the first English translation of the work appeared. This was 40 years after its original publication. Before that time, Febvre's work was really only known to experts in French history or to those who could read French.[5] The response was generally positive, and many felt that "Lucien Febvre was a man of very unusual and attractive powers of historical and psychological analysis."[6]

Febvre's methods were in tune with both the new ways in which historians were working and early twentieth-century socioeconomic developments. His focus on popular beliefs—shaped as they were by both economics and social trends—resonated in his own era. Historians and social scientists started investigating economics throughout the 1930s, in the wake of the worldwide economic depression that followed the Wall Street Crash* of 1929. In turn, economists started taking an interest in the social problems that came with the economic downturn, such as child poverty, falling standards of living, and price fluctuations.[7] Febvre's history of the sixteenth century appealed in an age when readers wanted to hear more about the general population.[8]

In response to this surge of interest, the *Annales* school formed one of a number of journals—including the British *Economic History Review*—that were founded at this time to promote the study of economic history.[9] Meanwhile, what was called progressive history* emerged in the US at this time. James Harvey Robinson,* F. J. Turner,* and Charles Beard* each worked on histories of social inequality and class divides.[10] Like Febvre, they fell in with circles of radical socialist* and liberal academics who wanted to reform society. Scholars refer to this as the new history in America, in the same way that historians in France termed *Annales* the new history.[11] Yet despite their similarities, the two operated in isolation.

The Problem of Unbelief appeared at the crest of a rising wave of change in historical studies. Even though it appeared in 1942, in the middle of World War II,* when academic history was obviously a low priority compared with the war effort, these underlying trends still made the book a success. Unable to fight because of his age (Febvre was 64 when *The Problem of Unbelief* was published), he was determined to keep the *Annales* periodical running and to continue working. Febvre despised the French Vichy* government that worked with the occupying Nazis,* but felt that as long as nothing else could be done, he should continue his work.[12]

Limitations

The Problem of Unbelief focuses on European history alone, exploring developments in the history of European religious thought, both inside and outside France. Yet while the scope of the book's subject matter was limited, Febvre's methodology was not. He intended the radical rethinking of historical method* he put forward in the book to be applied to any historical subject around the world. This was a global project that Febvre shared with Marc Bloch* and that was popularized by the *Annales* school.

There has been a lot of interest in Febvre's method, and historians in America, Britain, and Italy have taken up the methodological challenge. In Italy, Carlo Ginzburg* led the way for a microhistory* approach, effectively adopting a narrow lens to examine a well-defined single historical unit. This could be an event, a family, or even a person. Ginzburg looked at the religious views of a single miller, called Menocchio,* from Montereale in Italy.[13] Studying mentalities* and popular religious beliefs was also influential in both Britain and America in the 1960s and 1970s, with the most innovative American cultural historians today acknowledging their debt to Febvre.[14] However, no major historians outside Europe and America have taken up this method. European historians give lectures on the *Annales* school* in China and India, though, and *Annales* methods provide a useful contrast to the Marxist* approaches to history traditionally practiced there.[15] For the time being, some Western scholars use *Annales'* methods, while scholars in Asia, Africa, and beyond at least recognize the importance of these methods in Western historiography.[16]

NOTES

1   Peter Burke, *The French Historical Revolution: The Annales School, 1929–1989* (Stanford, CA: Stanford University Press, 1990), 28.

2   Marcel Bataillon, "Review of *La Religion de Rabelais*," *Mélanges d'Histoire Sociale* 5 (1944): 26.

3   Urban historian Louis Chevalier described them as this in a private letter to Fernand Braudel, dated June 3, 1960.

4   Paul Ricoeur, *Memory, History, Forgetting*, trans. Kathleen Blamey and David Pellauer (Chicago, IL: Chicago University Press, 2004), 544.

5   Joseph Tendler, *Opponents of the Annales School* (Basingstoke: Palgrave, 2013), 168.

6   H. O. Evennett, "Review of Lucien Febvre, *Au Coeur réligieux du XVIe siècle*," *English Historical Review* 73 (1958): 523.

7   Traian Stoianovich, *French Historical Method: The Annales Paradigm* (Ithaca, NY: Cornell University Press, 1976), 16.

8   Lucien Febvre, *The Problem of Unbelief in the Sixteenth Century*, trans. Beatrice Gottlieb (Cambridge, MA: Harvard University Press, 1982), 13.

9   Tendler, *Opponents of the Annales School*, 32.

10 Ernst A. Breisach, *American Progressive History: An Experiment in Modernization* (Chicago, IL: Chicago University Press, 1993), 117–29.

11 François Dosse, *L'Histoire en miettes: Des "Annales" à la "nouvelle histoire"* (History in pieces: From the «*Annales*» to the « new history») (Paris: Seuil, 1987).

12 André Burgière, *The Annales School: An Intellectual History*, trans. Jane Marie Todd (Ithaca, NY: Cornell University Press, 2009), 44–5.

13 Carlo Ginzburg, *The Cheese and the Worms: The Cosmos of a Sixteenth-Century Miller* (Baltimore, MD: Johns Hopkins University Press, 1980), 39.

14 Lynn Hunt, "French History in the Last Twenty Years: The Rise and Fall of the *Annales* Paradigm," *The Journal of Contemporary History* 21 (1986): 209–24.

15 Peter R. Campbell, "The New History: The *Annales* School of History and Modern Historiography," in *Historians and Historical Controversy*, ed. William Lamont (London: UCL Press, 1999), 17.

16 Peter Burke, "The *Annales* in Global Context," *International Review of Social History* 35 (1990): 421–32.

PLACE IN THE AUTHOR'S WORK

KEY POINTS

- Throughout his career, Febvre was interested in an understanding of popular religious attitudes through a thorough revision of historical practice.

- Febvre was intrigued by how sociologists first looked for facts, then tested the conclusions suggested by these facts. He felt historians simply researched facts, but didn't properly test their interpretations of how facts fitted together to form events.

- *The Problem of Unbelief* is considered to be Febvre's most important work in the history of ideas.*

Positioning

The Problem of Unbelief crowned Lucien Febvre's career when it was published in 1942, the year before his retirement. It developed the concept of mentality* first deployed by Febvre in his biography of the Reformation* theologian Martin Luther.* Like *The Problem of Unbelief*, Febvre's *Martin Luther: A Destiny* (published in 1928) analyzed the theology of a man in his context, moving from the beliefs of an individual to illuminate a wider mentality.[1] Febvre's intention was to show how religious historians and theologians actually made Luther's thought seem impenetrable, because they did not also study his thought in its own social context. He described the book as a "reminder" "not to impoverish excessively by brutal simplifications the nuanced richness of an oeuvre that was not melodic, but … polyphonic."[2] This work differed from a straightforward biography of Martin Luther because the focus was on popular religious beliefs

> ❝ Febvre's work played a major role in establishing what became for many an unquestionable dogma: that there was no atheism to be found in the sixteenth or even seventeenth centuries. ❞
>
> David Wootton, "Lucien Febvre and the Problem of Unbelief in the Early Modern Period"

situated in the context of an individual life, rather than a retelling of Luther's life as a great theologian. This meant that in his book Febvre not only uncovered new information through research, but also pioneered transformations of historical method* that were being investigated by the *Annales* school* more generally.

The way Febvre examined religious attitudes differed completely from that of his peers in the 1920s, as it would later in *The Problem of Unbelief*. At this time he was interested in the origins of the European Reformation, the period when the Protestant Church* broke away from the Roman Catholic Church* in Europe because of arguments about theology and worship. In *Martin Luther: A Destiny*, Febvre formed a "judgment on Luther" and his ideas by analyzing what Luther meant, and then placing it in the context of Christian thought during the Reformation.[3] Febvre found that both Rabelais* and Luther wanted to reform the Christian Church in order to unite its different factions under a renewed faith.

Integration

The Problem of Unbelief builds on a coherent attempt by Febvre throughout his career to reform the practice of historical writing in France and beyond, and to turn it into a rigorous, scientific discipline. In 1952, Febvre published a volume of essays he had written on this topic, entitled *Combats for History*.[4] The publication coincided with the death of his mentor, Henri Berr,* and Febvre used the occasion to group his essays into provocative sections headed: "Professions of faith at the outset," "Those for and against," "Alliances and supports," "The neighbors' views, or brothers who ignore," "Individuals and souvenirs," and "Hopes on arrival." Taken together, these titles set out a journey, from striving with the *Annales* school of 1929 to being celebrated as an international success by the 1950s. Febvre also borrowed the language of Reformation theologians such as Martin Luther to emphasize how the *Annales* school was itself reforming historical studies. Febvre did not impose this direction of reform artificially—the *Annales* had made these steps during his lifetime, albeit facing formidable opposition.

Febvre's efforts in this area began around 1900, while he was still a student, when he witnessed debates between social scientists and historians. The sociologist François Simiand* took a lead role in these robust debates, putting forward his theory that the discipline of sociology created general explanations by using a historical method. Sociologists compiled facts taken from evidence.[5] However, unlike historians, they generated and tested the general explanations to which these facts led. Historians, by contrast, assumed they must simply examine political facts. Sociologists used historical method with scientific precision. Historians did not.[6] Sociologists' empirical* examinations of groups of people, and their use of comparative methods to reach causal laws as explanations, gave them a scientific advantage over historians.[7] This, Simiand insisted, offered "objective" social scientists a "well-reasoned method" in reaction to the endless collection and recording of facts practiced by university historians such as Charles-Victor Langlois* and Claude Seignobos.*[8]

In *Combats for History*—and in *The Problem of Unbelief*—Febvre insisted on the need for a precise method of dealing with social facts. This gave him a coherent intellectual agenda with which to attempt a systematic revision of history writing.

Significance

Recognition for *The Problem of Unbelief* as Febvre's greatest work has grown steadily over time since its publication in 1942. This has been confirmed by the growing number of academic debates that have centered on its methods and conclusions, such as the work of David Wootton.*[9]

The book's effect on historical practice has proven so transformative that it is now considered to be Febvre's most significant study in the history of ideas. Contemporary scholars of historiography* and the history of religious attitudes have shown as much in their own work.[10] Although Febvre studied all areas of the history of religious beliefs in the sixteenth century—also looking at people who held anti-Christian beliefs—his conclusions about Rabelais and the impossibility that he could be an atheist* are best known, both for their simplicity and because subsequent research has not been able to fault them.

Scholars identify *The Problem of Unbelief* as a central text in the intellectual formation of the *Annales* school. Febvre's emphasis on the social aspects of mentality* became typical of later social history produced by the school. As an *Annales* sympathizer later explained, "The central hypothesis of *Le Problème de l'incroyance au XVIᵉ siècle* [The problem of unbelief] narrowly subordinates the individual's intellectual orientation to the conceptual framework of his time and society."[11] This proved significant not only for Febvre personally, but because it also inspired the work of other French historians who sought to place theological beliefs in their wider social contexts. Jacques Le Goff,* a member of the *Annales*, traced the changing concepts and views of purgatory,* while Philippe Ariès* identified shifting attitudes toward death.[12] This approach promoted close links between the history of ideas and social history, which became an important field of historical research for at least 40 years after the publication of *The Problem of Unbelief*, right up until the 1980s.[13]

NOTES

1   Lucien Febvre, *Martin Luther: Un Destin* (Martin Luther: A destiny) (Paris: Presses Universitaires de France, 1928).

2   Febvre, *Martin Luther*, vii.

3   Febvre, *Martin Luther*, i.

4   Lucien Febvre, *Combats pour l'histoire* (Combats for history) (Paris: Armand Colin, 1952).

5   François Simiand, "Méthode historique et science sociale: Étude critique d'après les ouvrages récents de M. Lacombe et de M. Seignobos" (Historical method and social science: A critical study in response to the recent works of Lacombe and Siegnobos), *Revue de Synthèse Historique* 2 (1902): 1–22; 128–77.

6   Simiand, "Méthode historique," 144; François Simiand, *La Méthode positive en science économique* (Positive method in economic science) (Paris: Alcan, 1912), 57, 80–1.

7   François Simiand, "La Causalité en histoire" (Causation in history), *Bulletin de la Société Française de Philosophie* 6 (1906): 252.

8   Simiand, "Méthode historique," 3, 143–4.

9   David Wootton, "Lucien Febvre and the Problem of Unbelief in the Early Modern Period," *Journal of Modern History* 6 (1988): 685–730; Nick Spencer, *Atheists: The Origin of the Species* (London: Bloomsbury, 2014), 18.

10 Marnie Hughes-Warrington, *Fifty Key Thinkers on History* (London: Routledge, 2000), 86.

11 André Burgière, *The Annales School: An Intellectual History*, trans. Jane Marie Todd (Ithaca, NY: Cornell University Press, 2009), 232.

12 Philippe Ariès, *L'Homme devant la mort* (The hour of our death) (Paris: Seuil, 1977); Jacques Le Goff, *La Naissance du purgatoire* (The birth of purgatory), trans. Arthur Goldhammer (Aldershot: Scolar Press, 1990).

13 Burgière, *The Annales School*, 244.

SECTION 3
IMPACT

MODULE 9
THE FIRST RESPONSES

KEY POINTS

- Critics of *The Problem of Unbelief* pointed out that Febvre ignored anti-Christian thinkers of the sixteenth century and questioned his conclusions about atheism.*

- Febvre never had the chance to respond to a number of these criticisms as they surfaced only after his death. But he defended his version of historical method* throughout his life.

- The relationship between history and the social sciences, combined with changes in French society, primarily shaped responses to *The Problem of Unbelief.*

Criticism

Lucien Febvre's *The Problem of Unbelief* was not heavily criticized when it was first published in 1942. This was because, to a large extent, scholarship was put on hold during World War II* and returned to pre-1939 levels only in the 1950s.

Criticism of Febvre's conclusion that atheism did not exist in the sixteenth century surfaced in the 1970s. French historian Jean Wirth* reopened the discussion regarding the role played by anti-Christian "free thinkers" in sixteenth-century France. Wirth tried to argue that free thinkers played a much greater role in the sixteenth century generally,[1] and in Strasbourg in particular,[2] than Febvre had thought. Suddenly, Febvre's judgment of Rabelais* seemed flawed.

French historian François Berriot* later challenged Febvre's findings regarding atheism in *The Problem of Unbelief* and in *Origène et Des Périers.** Febvre thought the term had no meaning for people

> **❝ A work by Lucien Febvre is always a lesson in method. That is the case whether it is a large book or article, whether the subject is Martin Luther or the origins of the French Reformation, or sixteenth-century unbelief, it is necessary to pose correctly, that is to say, historically, the historical questions. ❞**
>
> Marcel Bataillon, "Le Problème de l'incroyance au XVIᵉ siècle, d'après Lucien Febvre"

in the sixteenth century because they simply could not think outside the bounds of Christianity. Berriot, however, argued that the marginalized poor—and those alienated by the Church for other reasons, such as physical defects, independence of thought, or what was considered abnormal sexuality—may well have rejected a Christian God just as modern atheists do. Berriot thought Febvre was too quick to dismiss religious writers' uses of atheism, given the behavior of some of those who rejected God. Febvre centered his argument on the fact that it was impossible to think atheist thoughts and actually paid little attention to behavior.[3] In the view of his contemporaries, Berriot's work "added nuance" to that of Febvre, providing a brave revision of Febvre's widely accepted findings.[4] In addition, historian Jean-Jacques Denonain* reassessed the date of publication of notable anti-Christian texts such as *De tribus impostoribus*.[5] Because the genuine publication dates of such texts are still uncertain, the dates of the beginnings of atheist criticism remain so as well.

Responses

Berriot and Wirth's challenges to Febvre's thinking arose after Febvre's death, but during his lifetime he did respond to interpretations of sixteenth-century religious attitudes that he believed to be wrong.

French philosopher Étienne Gilson* studied the relationship between different bodies of medieval religious thought. He felt that, unlike medieval philosophers, twentieth-century thinkers had stopped forming moral judgments about the world around them. As a result, human beings no longer controlled events, but rather responded to them.[6] Febvre argued that Gilson misunderstood the development of ideas and that the concept of what science *was* differed greatly between the sixteenth and twentieth centuries. Philosophy had not become more scientific. Science itself meant something different.[7]

In the same year as *The Problem of Unbelief*, Febvre also published another book of his own on unbelief, *Origène et Des Périers*. This work performed a similar exercise in demonstrating the Christian points of reference that the French writer Bonaventure Des Périers* must have observed while writing his *Cymbalum Mundi*, which doubted the Christian faith.

Febvre continued to campaign for the *Annales* school* against its critics, defending the method he proposed in *The Problem of Unbelief*. He waged this campaign in the journal *Annales*, particularly in his reviews of other historians' works, attacking those that he believed used imprecise and unscientific methods. Febvre took issue with the work of constitutional historian Henri Jassemin* for simply charting the origins and development of political institutions without using any hypothesis to test his findings and without paying any attention to social history.[8]

Conflict and Consensus

The scholars Febvre attacked in *The Problem of Unbelief* came to terms with Febvre's argument, even though they had reached different conclusions. Henri Busson,* for example, adopted Febvre's idea of a mentality,* but he simply saw atheism as having a larger role than Febvre concluded. Yet Busson had previously consistently attacked

Febvre's work as unnecessarily argumentative, and as needlessly disrupting the established methods and findings of scholarship on religious attitudes.[9]

Social scientists, on the other hand, praised Febvre's contribution. Sociologist Jean Duvignaud* felt that Febvre helped develop the sociological method.[10] Similarly, Marcel Bataillon,* an expert in religious belief in seventeenth-century Spain, welcomed *The Problem of Unbelief* as an instructive example of historical method. Bataillon contributed a review of the volume to *Annales d'Histoire Sociale*, the journal edited by Febvre. In particular, Bataillon noted something that Febvre believed historical writing should achieve: explaining the past in its "living reality."[11] The tone of these reviews avoided conflict, which is unsurprising, given that both Duvignaud and Bataillon supported the *Annales* school. However, it is notable that they set aside Febvre's conclusions, since they likely felt more scholarship was needed to test them before they could comment.[12]

The dating of the adoption of anti-Christian beliefs by renowned figures such as Rabelais became symbolically significant in the twentieth century, because scholars wanted to prove the historical pedigree of secularism*—the separation of government institutions from the Church. Debates about Church–state relations in France lay behind these scholarly deliberations, which had divided French society in 1900. The Dreyfus Affair* of 1894 concerned allegations of treason against a young Jewish soldier, whom the courts eventually found innocent. Dreyfus's trials became public spectacles, and people took sides. Those eager to convict the Jewish soldier were often militant Catholics who wanted to destroy the French republic and restore the monarchy, spotting an opportunity to gain political capital by highlighting the vulnerability of France's political structure to attack. Republicans tended to emphasize that rational justice would prevail on the basis of the facts and that Dreyfus remained innocent until proven guilty.[13] Historians joined in the trials because judges asked them to act as expert witnesses about documentary evidence, upholding the neutrality of justice in the French Republic. Because of the political chaos ensuing from Dreyfus's trial, with all its religious undertones and intrigues, scholars after this time became convinced that public institutions—including education—should free themselves of religious signs and symbols.[14] Republicans and liberals in particular wished to claim the Enlightenment* as their intellectual origin, no matter what the historical truth was.[15]

NOTES

1   Jean Wirth, "'Libertins' et 'Epicuriens': Aspects de l'irréligion au XVIe siècle," ("Libertines" and "Epicureans": Aspects of irreligion in the sixteenth century), *Bibliothèque d'Humanisme et Renaissance* 29 (1977): 601–27.

2   Jean Wirth, *Croyants et sceptiques au XVIe siècle: Le Dossier des Epicuriens* (Believers and skeptics in the sixteenth century: The Epicurean file) (Strasbourg: Strasbourg University Press, 1981).

3   François Berriot, *Athéismes et athéistes au XVIe siècle en France* (Atheisms and atheists in sixteenth-century France, 2 vols.) (Lille: Lille University Press, 1985), 1:128–31.

4   Gabriel Audision, "Review of François Berriot, *Athéismes et athéistes au XVIe siècle en France*," *Revue d'Histoire des Religions* 203 (1986): 425.

5   Jean-Jacques Denonain, "Le Livre des trois imposteurs" (The book of three imposters), in *Aspects du libertinisme au XVIe siècle* (Aspects of sixteenth-century libertinism), ed. Marcel Bataillon (Paris: Albin Michel, 1974), 215–26.

6   Étienne Gilson, *Les Idées et les lettres: Essais d'art et de philosophie* (Ideas and literature: Essays on art and philosophy) (Paris: Vrin, 1932), 6–7.

7   Lucien Febvre, "Histoire des idées, histoire des sociétés: Une question de climat" (History of ideas, history of societies: A question of climate), *Annales. Histoire, Sciences Sociales* 2 (1946): 159.

8   Lucien Febvre, "Review of Henri Jassemin, *Le Chambre des Comptes de Paris*" (The Chamber of Accounts of Paris), *Annales d'histoire économique et sociale* 6 (1934): 148–53.

9   Suzanne Citron, "Positivisme, corporatisme et pouvoir dans la Société des Professeurs d'Histoire de 1910 à 1947" (Postivism, corporativism and power in the Society of History Professors from 1910 to 1947), *Revue Française de Science Politique* 27 (1977): 714–15.

10 Jean Duvignaud, "Review of Lucien Febvre, *Le Problème de l'incroyance au XVIe siècle. La Religion de Rabelais*," *L'Année Sociologique* 1 (1940): 454.

11 Lucien Febvre, *The Problem of Unbelief in the Sixteenth Century*, trans. Beatrice Gottlieb (Cambridge, MA : Harvard University Press, 1982), 26.

12 Bertrand Müller, *Lucien Febvre: Lecteur et critique* (Lucien Febvre: Reader and critic) (Paris: Albin Michel, 1994), 94.

13 Ruth Harris, *The Man on Devil's Island: Alfred Dreyfus and the Affair that Divided France* (London: Allen Lane, 2005), 218.

14 Madeleine Rebérioux, "Histoire, historiens et dreyfusisme" (History, historians and support for Dreyfus), *Revue Historique* 518 (1976): 407–9.

15 Rod Kedward, *La Vie en bleu: France and the French since 1900* (London: Allen Lane, 2005), 140.

THE EVOLVING DEBATE

KEY POINTS

- The understanding and use of mentalities* in *The Problem of Unbelief* and the conclusions Febvre drew promoted a study of popular religious belief that continues today.

- The *Annales* school* that Febvre helped found promoted collaboration between social scientists, as well as new research on subjects not previously studied by historians.

- *The Problem of Unbelief* and its methods have inspired scholars the world over.

Uses and Problems

Scholars developed the questions of religious attitude and method that Lucien Febvre raised in *The Problem of Unbelief* into the 1980s and 1990s. International travel enabled them both to meet each other at conferences and to gain access to foreign works.[1] By the 1980s, the *Annales* school had also acquired an international reputation thanks to the efforts of celebrated historian Fernand Braudel,* who used his international fame to publicize the school more widely, especially in the US and Italy.[2]

English historians of early-modern Britain such as Christopher Hill,* Gerald Aylmer,* and Michael Hunter* addressed the difficulties in identifying "atheism"* and anti-Christian thought in sixteenth- and seventeenth-century England.[3] These authors knew of *The Problem of Unbelief*, yet struggled to establish whether atheism could have been possible. Unlike Febvre, they preferred to look at the problem in general terms, focusing not on great individuals such as Rabelais,* but on society more broadly.

> **❝** The movement founded by Febvre and Bloch rapidly gained disciples and produced works of landmark significance, such as Febvre's *The Problem of Unbelief in the Sixteenth Century* and Bloch's masterpiece *Feudal Society*, published just at the outbreak of World War II. By the end of the war, *Annales*, now in Paris, had itself become the establishment in France, a position secured tightly in 1947 when Febvre became the founding president of the Sixth Section of the École Pratique des Hautes Études en Sciences Sociales, concerned with the social sciences, and the director of the Centre des Recherches Historiques within it. **❞**
>
> John W. O'Malley, *Trent and All That: Renaming Catholicism in the Early-Modern Era*

Following the example of social historians, religious historians also embraced a version of "history from below"* to look at popular piety.[4]

In France, the second generation of *Annales* scholars continued to reflect on the relationship between social structures and mentalities. Emmanuel Le Roy Ladurie,* often seen as an heir to Febvre and Braudel, amassed large quantities of statistical evidence to reconstruct the birthrate, climate, and farming practices of rural France in the sixteenth century, before then moving on to discuss the peasants' mentality.[5] Influenced by the work of the Italian Carlo Ginzburg,* Ladurie had also read inquisitorial records to identify the eccentric beliefs and intimate relations of a thirteenth-century village, Montaillou.[6] This fusion of social, cultural, and intellectual history has, however, been revised in recent years. Political history returned to prominence in the aftermath of the

Cold War* in the 1990s, following a period when members of the *Annales* school such as Jacques Le Goff* thought it had all but died out 20 years previously.[7] "Total history" changed once again and now became all-encompassing by including more space for the political dimension in the interdisciplinary study of past societies.

Schools of Thought

Febvre's bold, sometimes belligerent, claim for innovation in historical writing is still honored today. The journal he cofounded in 1929, *Annales*, continues under the full title *Annales. Histoire. Sciences Sociales*. This original group of historians effectively formed a school, since they all experimented with new forms of historical method.* Its members became "the most influential such school in twentieth-century historiography."[8] Leading books on history refer to the school, which demonstrates its continued relevance to the practice of history today.[9]

The *Annales* school has not focused only on connecting the history of ideas* to other subfields of history, such as social and economic history. It is true that economic and social history provided its earliest fields of specialization in the 1920s, and that in the 1930s it became known to international commentators as "the school of Lucien Febvre" or "Lucien Febvre's school."[10] Yet historians of all periods and areas of expertise—including medievalists, early-modern, and modern historians—joined. It is true to say, though, that medieval and early-modern historians predominated. Particularly in recent years, *Annales* has published articles developing new lines of historical thought with regard to gender, race, and ethnicity.[11] At its core—and despite many variations and new programs that have been launched since 1929—the *Annales* school remains committed to interdisciplinary study of all areas of the past, avoiding narrow specialization and unnecessary fragmentation in historical research.

In Current Scholarship

Febvre inspired generations of French historians from Michel Vovelle* to Jacques Le Goff to look closely at the mentality of populations in the past. Le Goff applied this to the history of religious thinkers in a manner similar to Febvre.[12] In France, the idea of mentality has become widely recognized by the general public since the work of Roger Chartier* and Michel Vovelle in the 1980s. Likewise, Le Goff's respected radio program "*Lundis de l'histoire*" (History Mondays) on the France Culture station brought the idea to a wider public, albeit one already interested in academic ideas.

Febvre's work on popular beliefs in sixteenth-century France has also been taken up by some prominent American scholars. Natalie Zemon Davis,* an American cultural historian of France, has engaged with Febvre in her work on sixteenth-century French culture. "He opened a historical–anthropological route of inquiry," Zemon Davis notes.[13] Other American historians such as Robert Darnton* have followed suit. His famous study of how, on one particular day, young printing apprentices in eighteenth-century Paris vented their frustrations with their impoverished lives by ritually killing cats echoes Febvre's methods. Darnton aims, like Febvre, to show that historians cannot easily explain past behavior that seems radically different from present standards. But with the help of anthropological models, historians can better investigate and explain peoples' mentalities.[14]

Febvre's international influence is also partly thanks to Roger Chartier's transatlantic career. Chartier has held university positions in France and America that allowed him to raise awareness of Febvre in both his teaching and his publications. His work has focused on the emergence of the book as one of the modern world's main forms of communicating information.[15] This work derived directly from projects begun by Febvre in the

1920s, in which he was able to explore sixteenth-century religious history precisely because the invention of the printing press—and so the book—happened during the Reformation* in the early sixteenth century.[16]

NOTES

1   Giuliana Gemelli, *Fernand Braudel*, trans. (into French) Brigitte Pasquet and Béatrice Propetto Marzi (Paris: Odile Jacob, 1995), 28.

2   Fernand Braudel, "Personal Testimony," *Journal of Modern History* 44 (1972): 448–67.

3   See, for example: Christopher Hill, "Irreligion in the Puritan Revolution," in *Radical Religion in the English Revolution*, ed. J. F. McGregor and Barry Reay (Oxford: Oxford University Press, 1984), 191–211.

4   David Wootton, "Lucien Febvre and the Problem of Unbelief in the Early Modern Period," *Journal of Modern History* 60 (1988): 721.

5   Emmanuel Le Roy Ladurie, *Les Paysans de Languedoc* (The peasants of Languedoc, 2 vols.) (Paris: SEVPEN, 1966), 1:11.

6   Emmanuel Le Roy Ladurie, *Montaillou: Village occitain de 1294 à 1324* (Montaillou: Languedoc village from 1294 to 1324) (Paris: Gallimard, 1975).

7   Jacques Le Goff, "Is Politics Still the Backbone of History?" *Daedalus: Journal of the American Academy of Arts and Sciences* 100 (1971): 1–19; Joseph Tendler, *Opponents of the Annales School* (Basingstoke: Palgrave, 2013), 70–1.

8   John Burrow, *A History of Histories. Epics, Chronicles, Romances & Inquiries from Herodotus and Thucydides to the Twentieth Century* (London: Allen Lane, 2007), 478.

9   Nancy Partner and Sarah Foot, eds., *The Sage Handbook of Historical Theory* (London: Sage, 2013).

10 Beatrice F. Hyslop, "Review of Bloch, *Apologie pour l'histoire*" (Apology for history), *American Historical Review* 55 (1950): 866–8, 868; A. J. P. Taylor, "Review of Renouvin, *Histoire des Relations Internationales*" (History of international relations), *English Historical Review* 70 (1955): 504.

11 André Burgière, *The Annales School: An Intellectual History*, trans. Jane Marie Todd (Ithaca, NY: Cornell University Press, 2009), 2.

12 Jacques Le Goff, *La Naissance du purgatoire* (The birth of purgatory), trans. Arthur Goldhammer (Aldershot: Scolar Press, 1990).

13 Natalie Zemon Davies and Denis Crouzet, *A Passion for History: Natalie Zemon Davies, Conversations with Denis Crouzet* (Kirksville, MO: Truman State University Press, 2010), 88.

14 Robert Darnton, *The Great Cat Massacre and Other Episodes in French Cultural History* (New York: Basic, 1984).

15 Roger Chartier, *Lectures et lecteurs dans la France d'Ancien Régime* (Paris: Seuil, 1987).

16 Lucien Febvre and Henri-Jean Martin, *L'Apparition du livre* (Paris: Albin Michel, 1957), xi.

IMPACT AND INFLUENCE TODAY

KEY POINTS

- Today, scholars regard *The Problem of Unbelief* as a classic text, a perfect example of the work of the Annales school* and very important to the study of Rabelais.*

- The mentalities* method continues to offer challenges to historian Alain Boureau* and philosopher Jean-Luc Cavaillé,* who believe scholars should restrict its use.

- Boureau, Cavaillé, and others see mentalities as producing histories that are too diluted to read when investigated without limits.

Position

Lucien Febvre's *The Problem of Unbelief* continues to be relevant because of its status as a classic work of history in the *Annales* tradition. Across the world, scholars refer to the text as having helped form the ideas behind the *Annales* school. Why? Because it combines the essential characteristics now associated with that school: interdisciplinary methods, new avenues of research (in this case, the social origins of belief), bold writing, and controversial conclusions.[1]

The book's position in religious history continues to stimulate research, meaning it is still part of current debates. The interdisciplinary characteristics both of Febvre's method and his conclusions still provoke responses from scholars across theology, philosophy, literature, and history. *The Problem of Unbelief* does not challenge one school of thought in particular. Rather, it poses questions to those working in the field of cultural studies and

> **❝** One of the greatest French historians of the twentieth century, Lucien Febvre, still, apparently, needs an introduction in the English-speaking world. **❞**
>
> Peter Burke, "Introduction: The Development of Lucien Febvre," in *The Annales School: Critical Assessments*

the study of popular culture in a range of disciplines.[2] That *The Problem of Unbelief* continues to prompt these questions means the book has stayed true to Febvre's original intention in writing it. He hoped in part to challenge scholars to find out the truth about sixteenth-century atheism* as much as he hoped to change how historians write history.

For these reasons the book remains a central element in the canon of history writing, providing both a benchmark by which to measure professional history generally, and a method for scholars of religious culture to engage with and confront it.

Interaction

Today, *The Problem of Unbelief* challenges scholars looking to limit the role of mentalities in historical and social and science research. Such limiting is something the medieval historian Alain Boureau and the sociologist Pierre Bourdieu* have tried to do, saying that scholars such as Febvre tended to make an impersonal mentality the operating cause of historical events.[3] Rather than unearthing a complete mentality, Boureau and Bourdieu tried to understand mentalities at particularly important moments of human decision-making. This meant that the way individuals and groups saw the world and how they then consciously decided to act became more important than it had been for Febvre. For Lucien Febvre, as for the French sociologist and anthropologist Lucien Lévy-Bruhl,* a mentality operated at a subconscious level.[4]

This new approach—based on the representations of reality that people made for themselves to communicate with each other in acceptable ways—focused on social customs. For example, social customs make it impolite to discuss money while eating dinner. Boureau and Bourdieu used this idea to show how a society's values determined human behavior.[5] Boureau in particular looks for interaction between "a determined social discourse and individual utterances."[6] For him, people behave in a way they think fits, depending on how they view their world. Febvre's idea of a mentality works the other way around: people in society behave in accordance with a subconscious mentality that they inherit from their peers. A pragmatic theory of language therefore suggests that societies force people to act in certain ways.

The Continuing Debate

The debate about sixteenth-century atheism and the correct historical method* required to find out what was true continues today, especially in France, and is not restricted to contributions from specialists in the sixteenth century. Instead, philosophers and literary scholars all take part in a debate about popular religious beliefs in Europe, although it is fair to say the debate continues largely within French university and research centers. Although national newspaper articles about secularism* in public institutions occasionally include such debates, they have become increasingly preoccupied with present concerns rather than taking a more historical perspective.[7]

The Problem of Unbelief challenges, first, those who argue that atheism began in the sixteenth century, using language theory as their method. The philosopher Jean-Pierre Cavaillé argues against Febvre, however, saying that language conventions determined what Rabelais could and could not say and what people would accept and what they would not. In other words, social customs embodied in language determine behavior, not mentalities. Social customs meant religion could be discussed only in a certain manner, and a line was drawn at criticizing the Church.[8] On the basis of this language theory, Cavaillé also argues that Febvre should not have used Lévy-Bruhl's theory of mentality for the sixteenth century. According to Cavaillé, because Lévy-Bruhl and Febvre worked in the twentieth century, they interpreted sixteenth-century thinking by the standard of logic prevalent in the twentieth century. In other words, Febvre's idea of problem-based* history was itself a twentieth-century lens that had not allowed him to properly understand the sixteenth century as he claimed. In this way of thinking, Febvre did the opposite of what he had intended. Cavaillé goes as far as to argue that readers can only ever understand Rabelais and his contemporaries such as Étienne Dolet* when they are read according to their own logic.[9]

Febvre's book also challenges intellectual historians who argued that pre-Christian religious thought influenced Rabelais and his peers. Febvre thought that pre-Christian and ancient thought played little part in the world Rabelais inhabited. He decided this after studying Rabelais's work in the context of his immediate contemporaries, the humanist* scholars. Much of Greek and Roman thought offered very different explanations as to the origins of the universe, and was indeed hostile to the "superstitions" of early Christians. Historian Marcel Picquier* found, however, that by looking more closely at Rabelais's contemporaries—Étienne Dolet, for example—it becomes clear that ancient thought did feature heavily in the sixteenth century after all. So anti-Christian ideas and atheism played a larger role in the production of literature of the period.[10] In that sense, Febvre had used his method too narrowly and reached the wrong conclusions.

NOTES

1   André Burgière, *The Annales School: An Intellectual History*, trans. Jane Marie Todd (Ithaca, NY: Cornell University Press, 2009), 23.

2   Jean-Loup Kastler, "Du 'problème de l'incroyance' à 'l'étrange liberté': Un changement de paradigme de l'histoire des expériences religieuses?" (From "the problem of unbelief" to "the strange liberty": A change of paradigm in the history of religious experiences), *Théorèmes* 5 (2013): 63–82.

3   François Dosse, *Empire of Meaning: The Humanization of the Human Sciences*, trans. Hassan Melehy (Minneapolis: Minnesota University Press, 1999), 229–30.

4   Pierre Bourdieu, *La Distinction: Critique sociale du jugement* (Distinction: A social critique of the judgment of taste) (Paris: Minuit, 1979), 5–7; Alain Boureau, *La Droit de cuissage: Fabrication d'un mythe (XIIIᵉ–XXᵉ siècle)* (The lord's first night: The myth of the «right of the thigh») (Paris: Albin Michel, 1995), 4–12.

5   Alain Boureau, *En somme. Pour un usage analytique de la scolastique médiévale (In total. For an analytical usage of medieval scholarship) (Lagrasse:* Verdier, 2011); Pierre Bourdieu, *La Distinction*.

6   Boureau, *La Droit de cuissage*, 230.

7   Stéphane Le Bars, "Les Revendications identitaires sont inquiétantes: Le Président de l'Observatoire de la laïcité défend une conception du combat laïque qui va au-delà de la loi de 1905" (Claims about identity cause concern: The president of the Secular Observatory defends an illegal vision of secular combat that continues outside of the law of 1905), *Le Monde*, July 4, 2010, 8.

8   Jean-Pierre Cavaillé, "Les Frontières de l'inacceptable. Pour un réexamen de l'histoire de l'incrédulité" (The frontiers of the unacceptable: Toward a re-examination of the history of unbelief), *Les Dossiers du Grihl,* accessed October 20, 2014, http://dossiersgrihl.revues.org/4746; doi: 10.4000/ dossiersgrihl.4746.

9   Cavaillé, "Les Frontières."

10 Marcel Picquier, *Étienne Dolet (1509–1546): Imprimeur humaniste lyonnais mort sur le bûcher* (Étienne Dolet (1509–1546): Humanist printer of Lyons dead on the pyre) (Lyons: Association laïque lyonnaise des Amis d'Étienne Dolet, 2009), 16–39.

MODULE 12
WHERE NEXT?

KEY POINTS

- *The Problem of Unbelief* will continue to be regarded as a classic of Annales history.

- Febvre's conclusion that atheism* remained impossible in the sixteenth century looks set to be debated for decades to come as researchers continue to investigate popular religious beliefs in early-modern Europe.

- The book is groundbreaking because it transformed understandings of sixteenth-century popular religious belief, while acting as a perfect example of the contribution of the Annales school* to the practice of history.

Potential

Lucien Febvre's *The Problem of Unbelief* will remain a foundational text in ongoing debates about the right way to interpret sixteenth-century literature. Reviews of writings on this often-debated topic always begin with Febvre's work before going on to evaluate later interpretations.[1] Even those with something new to say about sixteenth-century atheism still converse directly with Febvre's work, whether to reject his conclusions or to critique his method in the light of their own. This trend seems set to continue, given both the ongoing uncertainty about exactly what religious belief in the sixteenth century was, and the ongoing importance of religion in contemporary military, social, and cultural conflicts.[2] Debates about how the state can best interact with and promote freedom of religion will make sure Febvre remains relevant.

> ❝Whether there were atheists, in the sense of people who did not believe in God, in early-modern Europe has been the subject of a significant historical debate since 1942 when Lucien Febvre published a major study entitled *The Problem of Unbelief in the Sixteenth Century.*❞
>
> Nick Spencer, *Atheists: The Origin of the Species*

Febvre's name and work will also remain embedded in historical scholarship because of its fundamental connection to the inspirational *Annales* school. The school features in most articles and books about modern historiography,* be they from a national, European, or international perspective.[3] And historians continue to take inspiration from the *Annales* as they attempt to write global histories.

Future Directions

A growing number of European historians are using *Annales* methods to write about world history, particularly in Berlin, where historians have adopted the global ambitions of the *Annales* school.[4] Young historians such as Sebastian Conrad* combine Febvre's interest in early-modern topics such as the Enlightenment* with radical methods proposed by the *Annales* school. Conrad aims to write a global history of the Enlightenment, combining Western perspectives with those of people in Asia and Africa. This will build on his earlier comparative history of imperial Germany and Japan, itself styled on Marc Bloch* and Febvre's preference for regional histories that compare areas in two or more different countries.[5]

The *Annales* still have a wider influence on how scholars teach history, even if the school does not dominate in the way it did in the 1990s.[6] The historian David Christian* has formulated the idea of Big History, which teaches students to look at a far-ranging overview of history.[7] Christian's idea, like Febvre's, insists that only when readers have an overview of a subject can they fully understand its parts. The works of *Annales* historians inspired Christian to take up this project, which has now come to the attention of American IT entrepreneur Bill Gates,* who wants Big History to feature prominently in American classrooms.[8] Equally, university historians have returned to considering the idea of global and total history that was familiar to Henri Berr* and Febvre, as well as to Fernand Braudel* and the *Annales* school more generally. The 2014 open-access publication *The History Manifesto* again asks what importance we attach to history teaching and urges historians to return to the study of the long-term past over 500 years, avoiding over-specialization and separation between the social sciences. Just as Febvre did, it urges historians to involve themselves and put their skills at the disposal of both governments and the general public.[9]

Other future studies and projects basing themselves on the *Annales* school and on Febvre's work in *The Problem of Unbelief* will likely follow in the path of these grand designs. This should not be surprising. Febvre and his colleagues never shrank away from ambitious new projects.

Summary

The Problem of Unbelief is not an obscure text about sixteenth-century religious ideas. Rather, its author and its pages gave history radical new methods and provided a new interpretation of sixteenth-century atheism that is still controversial and contested today. Contemporary scholars such as André Burgière* say that Febvre's student Fernand Braudel* is the most important historian of the twentieth century.[10] However, without Febvre the intellectual innovation of the *Annales* school would not have happened, and Braudel would not have embarked on the project about Mediterranean history that made him famous.[11]

Both Febvre's interdisciplinary method and his range of sources give *The Problem of Unbelief* its continuing appeal. It defies simple categorization as a history book, given the ongoing debate among scholars of different subjects about sixteenth-century religious beliefs. Whether readers agree or disagree with Febvre, or whether they like or dislike his writing style, *The Problem of Unbelief* is an invaluable introduction to the nature of historical writing and to the basic concepts that history students will encounter, such as anachronism* and change over time. Without Febvre's contribution, histories written today would look very different, and the *Annales* school* probably would not have attained the international success it still enjoys.

" "

NOTES

1   Jean-Loup Kastler, "Du 'problème de l'incroyance' à 'l'étrange liberté': Un changement de paradigme de l'histoire des expériences religieuses?" (From "the problem of unbelief" to "the strange liberty": A change of paradigm in the history of religious experiences?), *Théorèmes* 5 (2013): 63–82.

2   See for example: Anthony Grafton, *Cardano's Cosmos: The Worlds and Works of a Renaissance Astrologer* (Cambridge, MA: Harvard University Press, 2001).

3   Georg G. Iggers and Edward Wang, *A Global History of Modern Historiography* (London: Routledge, 2008), 186.

4   Jürgen Kocka, "Comparison and Beyond," *History and Theory* 42 (2003): 39–44.

5   Sebastian Conrad, "Enlightenment in Global History: A Historiographical Critique," *American Historical Review* 117 (2012): 999–1027; Sebastian Conrad, *The Quest for the Lost Nation: Writing History in America and Japan in the American Century*, trans. Alan Nothnagle (Berkeley: University of California Press, 2010), 30, 70–1, 156.

6   Peter Burke, *The French Historical Revolution: The Annales School 1929–1989* (Stanford, CA: Stanford University Press), 2.

7   See the website: https://www.bighistoryproject.com/home.

8   Andrew Ross Sorkin, "So Bill Gates Has this Idea for a History Class," *New York Times*, September 5, 2014, accessed October 30, 2014, http://www.nytimes.com/2014/09/07/magazine/so-bill-gates-has-this-idea-for-a-history-class.html?_r=1.

9   Jo Guldi and David Armitage, *The History Manifesto* (Cambridge: Cambridge University Press, 2014), 125; also available via open access: http://historymanifesto.cambridge.org/files/4714/1880/4698/historymanifesto.pdf.

10   André Burgière, *The Annales School: An Intellectual History*, trans. Jane Marie Todd (Ithaca, NY: Cornell University Press, 2009), x–xii.

11   Fernand Braudel, *The Mediterranean and the Mediterranean World in the Age of Philip II of Spain*, trans. Sîan Reynolds (New York: Harper & Row, 1972).

GLOSSARIES

GLOSSARY OF TERMS

Anachronism: an error of chronology, when any item, person, or phrase appears in a period in which it does not belong. For example, Febvre says it is anachronistic to discuss sixteenth-century atheism as it was not possible to think outside a Christian frame of mind at that time.

***Annales* school:** a group of French historians and social scientists who gathered around the journal *Annales d'Histoire Économique et Sociale* (Annales of Social and Economic History), founded by March Bloch* and Lucien Febvre in 1929.

Atheism: the broad refusal to believe in the existence of any gods, whether Christian or otherwise.

Cold War: usually dated from 1947 until 1991, this was a long period of tension and enmity between Eastern and Western powers and, in particular, between the Soviet Union and the United States.

Communism: an economic doctrine that argues that there should be no private ownership of the means of production (natural resources, factories, capital such as machines). Instead, working people should own the means of production, and the government they create should plan economic output to meet the needs of all workers.

Dreyfus Affair: a political scandal focusing on the trials between 1894 and 1906 of Alfred Dreyfus (1859–1935) on charges of espionage. Monarchist Catholics hoped to seize on the trial as symptomatic of the weakness of the French government and strengthen the case to bring back the monarchy, while republicans believed impartial justice would be done and Dreyfus would be tried on the facts alone.

Empiricism/Empirical approach: the idea that all knowledge should be gained by experience, by using experiments and observation to gather facts.

Enlightenment: a period from the end of the seventeenth into the eighteenth century when intellectuals, especially in France, re-evaluated their knowledge of the world around them using the latest techniques of experimental science and rational thought.

Epistemology: the branch of philosophy that considers how the human mind acquires knowledge of the world around it, what knowledge is true and what is opinion, and the extent to which people can know about objects and people they encounter.

French Revolution: a period of political and social upheaval in France that began in 1789 with the popular overthrow of the monarchy and ended in 1799 with the rise of Napoleon.

Historical method: a method of investigation in which the historical factors relevant to a particular situation or phenomenon are studied. Historians disagree about how best to interrogate past people and events in order to discover the truth about them.

Historiography: the study of historians' ways of researching and writing about the past. It looks at historical method and at historical understanding, and the evidence on which historians rely, as well as examining historians' own influences and ideas.

History from below: the study of past events from the perspective of people not previously included in political and constitutional narratives, such as women, rural laborers, watchmakers, and servants.

History of ideas: a subdiscipline of historical research in which historians investigate the expression, presentation, and change of human ideas over time.

Humanism: a collection of sixteenth-century beliefs emphasizing the importance of reviving and re-examining the work of classical authors who wrote in Latin. Humanist scholars looked to revitalize Christian scholarship and the Christian Church by learning from the classical Greek and Roman authors.

Kantianism: based on the works of the German philosopher Immanuel Kant (1724–1804), Kantianism encompasses a range of subjects, focusing on how the human mind can analyze and know about the world around it.

Marxist: an approach to historical study or any other pursuit based on Marxism, the body of work produced by Karl Marx (1818–83), explaining events in all aspects of life as the result of economic forces that determined human behavior.

Mentality/mental tools: the study of the subconscious notions and concepts by which past peoples view the world around them. For example, scholars such as Lucien Lévy-Bruhl* argued that there existed a primitive and a Western mentality—the latter insisted on civil society and civilization as virtues, the former on survival.

Microhistory: a practice of historians, developed by Carlo Ginzburg.* It requires the close study of a small area, event, or individual, in order to generalize about the society in which that area, event, or individual features. An example would be the study of the life of a craftsman in order to work out his views on God, and then to generalize from that to competing popular religious beliefs.

Nazi government: the government of Germany between 1933 and 1945, led by Adolf Hitler. It promoted a collection of beliefs, including the assertion of Aryan racial superiority and the expansion of the German state.

Problem history: an approach to historical research developed by *Annales* historians (*histoire problème* in French) that identifies unexplained aspects of the present and provides a historical explanation of their origins using a rigorous, interdisciplinary historical method.

Progressive history: the movement begun in the US by Charles Beard,* James Harvey Robinson,* and others to promote the study of ordinary Americans using a combination of economic, social, and cultural evidence analyzed historically in order to highlight the ongoing need for social reform to improve the lives of the majority of working Americans.

Protestant Church: a branch of the Christian Church founded during the Reformation and devoted to the teachings of Protestantism and the practice thereof.

Protestantism: a system of religious ideas formulated during the Reformation to correct perceived errors in the teachings of the Roman Catholic Church. Principal among these ideas is the notion that the Eucharistic bread is not the body of Christ but a *representation* of the body of Christ.

Purgatory: according to the Roman Catholic Church, purgatory is where those who prove worthy to ascend to heaven after death go in order to be cleansed so that they are ready to enter heaven.

Rationalism: the doctrine or belief that reason should be the only guiding principle in life, removing the need for reliance on, or adherence to, any form of religious belief.

Reformation: a movement beginning in Europe in the early sixteenth century, and around 1517 by Martin Luther in Germany. The Reformation began as a result of disputes over the teachings and practices of the Roman Catholic Church, and a separated, reformed church emerged. The Protestant Church still exists today.

Renaissance: an intellectual and artistic movement that began in fourteenth-century Europe and ended in the seventeenth century. It witnessed the birth of new, technical approaches in art, educational reform, laboratory-style methods in science, and the formulation of diplomatic and legal conventions.

Republicanism: a form of government characterized by the active role played by citizens and the establishment of institutions that aim to combat corruption and promote the rule of law. Most importantly, the head of the government is not selected by rules of heredity, but by other means, most commonly through elections.

Roman Catholic Church: the branch of the Christian Church led by the Pope, the head of the Roman Catholic Church in Vatican City, Rome.

Secularism: the principle of the separation of national institutions of government from the Church and religious leaders. The motivation for free thought and rationalism to prevail in public affairs stems from this principle.

Socialism: the collection of economic and social principles that insist a country's natural resources and factories should be owned by the people communally, rather than by private individuals, and that the proceeds of economic activity should be applied equally for the benefit of everybody.

Soviet Union: also known as the Union of Soviet Socialist Republics (USSR), this was an alliance between nations centering on Russia, which existed between 1917 and 1991, with communism as its system of government.

Theology: the academic or learned study of God, religious studies, and systems of religious belief.

Theory of relativity: theory devised by German-born physicist Albert Einstein (1879–1955), which stated that the universe had five dimensions: length, breadth, width, space, and time.

USSR: see Soviet Union.

Vichy France: the name of the French government between 1940 and 1944 that collaborated with the Nazi government during its occupation of France in World War II.

Wall Street Crash: the worst financial crisis in American and world history prior to the 2008 financial crash. It began in October 1929, when investors who had overstretched themselves on the mistaken belief that they would benefit from the gains of their investment found themselves penniless as prices plummeted amid financial panic.

World War I: the armed conflict lasting from 1914 until 1918 between the key Central Powers of Austria-Hungary, Germany, and Italy and the Allied Powers—the British Empire, France, and the Russian Empire—on whose side the United States also fought after joining the war. Because many participating powers had colonial territories, the war spread across the globe.

World War II: the worldwide armed conflict lasting from 1939 until 1945 (with some variation, depending on the country concerned), beginning with the German invasion of Poland. The United States later entered the war when Germany's allies, the Japanese, attacked a US naval base at Pearl Harbor.

PEOPLE MENTIONED IN THE TEXT

Charles Andler (1866–1933) was a French scholar of German and philosophy, best known for his work on German state socialism, *Les Origines du socialisme d'état en Allemagne* (The origins of state socialism in Germany).

Philippe Ariès (1914–84) was a French medievalist influenced intellectually by the right-wing group Action Française (French Action). After World War II, he also became closely linked with historians on the left and wrote classic works on childhood, family structures, and notions of death, partly under the influence of the *Annales* school.*

Gerald Aylmer (1926–2000) was an English historian and specialist in early-modern history. His famous studies include *The Crown's Servants: Government and Civil Service under Charles II 1660–85*.

Mikhail Bakhtin (1895–1975) was a Russian writer and literary critic who wrote on many topics, including Rabelais.* His work *Rabelais and His World* (1984, originally published in Russian in 1965) focuses on the role of carnival and exaggeration in Rabelais's work.

Victor Basch (1863–1944) was a Hungarian-born Germanist, both a professor of Germanist studies at the Sorbonne and a politician in France. Febvre knew of him from his studies of German writers and philosophers; for example, *Essai d'esthétique de Kant* (Essay on the aesthetics of Kant).

Marcel Bataillon (1895–1977) was a French expert on Spain, with particular expertise in the spirituality of sixteenth-century Spain. He was also well known for his studies of the theologian Erasmus.*

Charles Beard (1874–1948) was an American social historian and political activist. He was best known for his understanding of the American constitution as an act of economic self-interest, *An Economic Interpretation of the Constitution of the United States* (1913).

Henri Berr (1863–1954) was a French schoolteacher and philosopher who founded the *Revue de Synthèse Historique* (The review of historical synthesis), where Febvre worked.

François Berriot (b. 1939) is a French historian of literature and religious thought, with a particular interest in atheism.*

Marc Bloch (1886–1944) was a medieval historian and a member of the French Resistance who fought against the German occupation of France during World War II. He founded the *Annales* school* together with Lucien Febvre and wrote famous works such as *La Société féodale* (Feudal society).

Pierre Bourdieu (1930–2002) was a French sociologist whose work looked at the role of power and social status in societies and the way people interact as a result. His best-known text is *Distinction: A Social Critique of the Judgment of Taste.*

Alain Boureau (b. 1946) is a French medieval historian who now directs the École des Hautes Études en Sciences Sociales (EHESS) that Febvre helped to found in 1947. His area of expertise concerns the history of Christianity and Roman Catholicism.

Fernand Braudel (1902–85) was a historian of early-modern Europe, the Mediterranean, and North Africa. He is best known for his 1949 work *La Méditerranée et le monde méditerranéen à l'époque de Philippe II* (The Mediterranean and the Mediterranean world in the age of Philip II of Spain).

André Burgière is a French historian of French cultural and social history. He served as secretary to the *Annales*, the journal Febvre and Marc Bloch* founded in 1929, and studied the intellectual history of the school in his book *The Annales School* (2006).

Henri Busson (1870–1946) was a historian and geographer of early-modern France, famous for *Les Sources et le développement du rationalisme dans la littérature française de la Renaissance, 1533–1601* (The sources and development of rationalism in Renaissance French literature).

Jean-Pierre Cavaillé (b. 1959) is a French philosopher who graduated from the École des Hautes Études en Sciences Sociales (EHESS) that Febvre helped found in 1947. He currently teaches philosophy there, where he has been a professor since 2013.

Roger Chartier (b. 1945) is a French historian of early-modern France and a specialist in the history of the written word and books. He is currently a professor in Paris and at the University of Pennsylvania, USA.

David Christian (b. 1946) is an Anglo-American historian who specializes in the history of Russia. In 1989, he taught the first ever module on Big History, teaching students an overview of past events rather than taking events in turn in microscopic detail.

Sebastian Conrad (b. 1978) is a German historian of transnational and global history, and professor of history at the Free University, Berlin. He has written on the ways in which nations redefine and attempt to claim their history in the wake of military defeat, as for example in *The Quest for the Lost Nation*.

Robert Darnton (b. 1939) is an American historian, librarian, and specialist in French history and literature, currently Carl H. Pforzheimer university professor at Harvard University. His notable recent works include *Censors at Work: How States Shaped Literature*.

Natalie Zemon Davis (b. 1928) is an American-born historian of France and Europe during the early-modern period. Among her works that combine imaginative writing with scholarly research is *The Return of Martin Guerre* (1983).

Jean-Jacques Denonain was a French historian of early-modern French religious and cultural history.

René Descartes (1596–1650) was a French philosopher and mathematician whose work now assumes a central place as the keystone of rational Western philosophy.

Étienne Dolet (1509–46) was a French writer, printer, and philologist. It is widely disputed whether Dolet's thought should fall into the Protestant camp or the rationalist anti-Christian camp of Descartes.

Georges Duby (1919–96) was a French historian of medieval Europe whose work focused on the social and economic history of that period. Among his celebrated cultural histories is *The Legend of Bouvines* (published in French in 1973 and translated under this title in 1990).

Émile Durkheim (1858–1917) was a French sociologist and social psychologist, widely regarded as having founded the modern discipline of sociology. Among his best-known works is *Les Règles de la méthode sociologique* (The rules of the sociological method).

Jean Duvignaud (1921–2007) was a French novelist and sociologist, as well as a secondary school teacher, and university professor at the University of Tours.

Albert Einstein (1879–1955) was a German-born physicist who revolutionized physics with his general theory of relativity. This stated that the universe had five dimensions: length, breadth, width, space, and time.

Desiderius Erasmus (1466–1536) was a Dutch philosopher and priest. He and Martin Luther debated the best ways to reform the Church as part of the Reformation.

Anatole France (1844–1924) was a French poet, journalist, and novelist, who spent his working life in Paris. He won the Nobel Prize for literature in 1921.

Bill Gates (b. 1955) is an American IT entrepreneur best known for founding the Microsoft Corporation in 1975 at the age of 20.

Giovanni Gentile (1875–1944) was a Sicilian-born philosopher who worked in the tradition of the German philosopher G. W. F. Hegel to provide an overall picture of man's place, past and future, in the world.

Étienne Gilson (1884–1978) was a French historian of philosophy whose early work focused on Descartes.* Among his better-known works is *L'Être et l'essence* (Being and essence).

Carlo Ginzburg (b. 1939) is an Italian historian of early-modern Europe and the Reformation, noted for his historical topics in an interdisciplinary framework using a variety of sources, from art to scientific manuals. He is best known for his 1980 work, *The Cheese and the Worms*, original published in Italy as *Il formaggio e i vermi* in 1976.

Christopher Hill (1912–2003) was an English historian of early-modern England who furthered a Marxist interpretation of the past, explaining social and political developments with reference to the economic conditions under which they occurred. His best-known works focused on early-modern English history, as in *The World Turned Upside Down: Radical Ideas During the English Revolution.*

Michael Hunter (b. 1949) is an English historian working at Birkbeck College, University of London. He has edited Boyle's *Works* and *Correspondence*, all appearing between 1999 and 2001.

Henri Jassemin (1893–1935) was a French medieval historian and specialist in the constitutional and administrative development of France.

Charles-Victor Langlois (1863–1929) was an archivist and medieval historian, as well as a specialist in historical method. He is most famous for the work on historical method he wrote with modern historian Charles Seignobos, *Introduction aux études historiques* (Introduction to historical method).

Abel Lefranc (1863–1952) was a French historian of literature specializing in modern French literary history since the Renaissance.

Jacques Le Goff (1924–2014) is a French medieval historian and member of the *Annales* school. Le Goff's work continues in the vein of Febvre's on medieval Christianity, of which *Intellectuals of the Middle Ages* (1993; originally published in French in 1957) is a key example.

Robert Lenoble (1902–59) was a French priest, ordained in 1925, and a historian of science and philosophy. He is particularly noted for his study of the relations between religious and scientific thought, as in *Esquisse d'une histoire de l'idée de nature* (Outline of a history of the idea of nature).

Emmanuel Le Roy Ladurie (b. 1929) is a French historian of France during the early-modern period, with a particular interest in the French peasantry of that era. Among his best-known works are 1966's *Les Paysans de Languedoc* (The peasants of Languedoc).

Lucien Lévy-Bruhl (1857–1939) was a French philosopher who worked in the fields of sociology, anthropology, and ethnology, as well as philosophy. He is best known for his 1910 study of primitive tribes, *How Natives Think*.

Arthur O. Lovejoy (1873–1962) was a German-born American historian of ideas and intellectual history. He remains famous as a pioneer of the history of ideas in America.

Martin Luther (1483–1546) was a German theologian. The German Reformation began when he hammered his 95 theses about the need to reform Catholicism to a church door in Wittenberg.

Menocchio/Domenico Scandella (1532–99) was a miller from Montereale, Italy. His philosophical teachings earned him a reputation as heretical during the Reformation, as a result of which he was burned at the stake. His life and beliefs were the subject of Carlo Ginzburg's *The Cheese and the Worms*.

Jules Michelet (1798–1874) was a French historian of the history of France, particularly since the Renaissance, which Michelet saw as the beginning of modern France.

Gabriel Monod (1844–1912) was a French historian of modern France and historiography, who founded France's leading scholarly journal for history, the *Revue Historique* (Historical review). Among his best-known works is *Renan, Taine, Michelet: Les Maîtres d'histoire* (Renan, Taine and Michelet: Masters of history).

Bonaventure des Périers (1510–1544) was a French author who received royal patronage for his free inquiry into the nature of religion. His 1537 work, *Cymbalum Mundi*, caused controversy because it put forward a skeptical view of Christianity that challenged accepted norms.

Marcel Picquier (b. 1930) is French historian and specialist in the Renaissance publishing industry and religious thought.

René Pintard (1883–1938) was a French historian of popular religious belief—including free thinkers, or so-called libertines—in seventeenth-century France. His work *Le Libertinage érudit dans la première moitié du XVIIᵉ siècle* (Learned libertinism in the first half of the seventeenth century) (1943) coincided with *The Problem of Unbelief*, both in terms of publication and subject.

François Rabelais (1483–1553) was a French humanist and Renaissance writer, who was born in western France and died in Paris. Rabelais's best-known work remains his novel *Gargantua and Pantagruel*.

Paul Ricoeur (1913–2005) was a French philosopher best known for his work on hermeneutics, the philosophical method by which philosophers and other scholars determine a document's meaning. He had a distinguished career in France, first in Rennes and then in Paris, and was also well known in the United States.

James Harvey Robinson (1863–1936) was an American historian of US social and intellectual history, as well as European history.

Bertrand Russell (1872–1970) was an English philosopher, mathematician, and political activist. One of the greatest logicians of the twentieth century, he formulated a system of thought built around logical principles rather than vague, literary notions that led him to renounce Christian belief in *Why I Am Not a Christian and Other Essays on Religion and Related Subjects*.

Claude Seignobos (1854–1942) was a French historian of French and European history, as well as historical theory. He is best remembered for his introduction to the 1898 historical method textbook, coauthored with Charles-Victor Langlois, *Introduction aux études historiques* (Introduction to historical studies).

François Simiand (1873–1935) was a French economist and social scientist who campaigned for social scientists, including historians, to use scientific methods in their work.

Lynn Thorndike (1882–1965) was an American historian of religion and science, who spent the majority of his career at the prestigious Columbia University in New York City. His early work bears on Febvre's own research, especially 1905's *The Place of Magic in the Intellectual History of Europe*.

Louis Thuasne (1854–1940) was a Paris-born specialist in medieval French and Renaissance literature. He made his reputation through studying archival sources on the evolution of the French language.

Frederick Jackson Turner (1861–1932) was an American historian of modern US social and economic history and a specialist on the formation of the modern United States in the nineteenth century. His most famous work remains *The Significance of the Frontier in American History* (1893).

Voltaire, né Francois-Marie Arouet (1694–1778) was a French writer and Enlightenment thinker. His work satirically addresses religious and other forms of intolerance and narrow-mindedness.

Michel Vovelle (b. 1933) is a French historian of modern European history, who occupied the Chair for the History of the French Revolution at the Sorbonne prior to his retirement. His notable works include *La Mentalité révolutionnaire: Société et mentalités sous la Révolution française* (Revolutionary mentality: Society and mentality under the French Revolution).

Max Weber (1864–1920) was a German sociologist, philosopher, and legal scholar. He is best known for his study of the relationship between religion and economic thought in modern Europe, as in 1905's *Die protestantische Ethik und der Geist des Kapitalismus* (The Protestant ethic and the spirit of capitalism).

Jean Wirth (b. 1947) is a French historian and specialist in medieval art, a professor at the Sorbonne, at the University of Illinois in the US, and in Strasbourg. Recent work include 2011's *L'Image à la fin du Moyen Âge* (Icons at the end of the Middle Ages).

David Wootton is a British historian of the intellectual and cultural history of English-speaking nations, France, and Italy between 1500 and 1800. He is currently anniversary professor of history at York University in the United Kingdom; one of his more recent books is *Galileo: Watcher of the Skies* (2011).

WORKS CITED

WORKS CITED

Ariès, Philippe. *L'Homme devant la mort* (The hour of our death). Paris: Seuil, 1977.

Audision, Gabriel. "Review of François Berriot, *Athéismes et athéistes au XVIe siècle en France*" (Atheisms and atheists in sixteenth-century France). *Revue d'Histoire des Religions* 203 (1986): 425.

Bataillon, Marcel. «Le Problème de l'incroyance au XVIe siècle, d'après Lucien Febvre.» *Mélanges d'Histoire Sociale* 5 (1944): 5–26.

———. "Review of *La Religion de Rabelais.*" *Mélanges d'Histoire Sociale* 5 (1944): 26.

Berr, Henri. *La Synthèse en histoire*. Paris: Albin Michel, 1911.

Berriot, François. *Athéismes et athéistes au XVIe siècle en France* (Atheisms and atheists in sixteenth-century France, 2 vols.). Vol. 1, 128–31. Lille: Lille University Press, 1985.

Bloch, Marc. «Méthodologie historique.» Unpublished notes.

———.*The Royal Touch: Sacred Monarchy and Scrofula in England and France*. Translated by J. E. Anderson. London: Routledge, 1973; originally published in France in 1924.

———. *La Société féodale* (Feudal society, 2 vols.). Paris: Albin Michel, 1939–40.

Bourdieu, Pierre. *La Distinction: Critique sociale du jugement* (Distinction: A social critique of the judgment of taste). Paris: Minuit, 1979.

Boureau, Alain. *La Droit de cuissage: Fabrication d'un mythe (XIIIe–XXe siècle)* (The lord's first night: The myth of the "right of the thigh"). Paris: Albin Michel, 1995.

———. *En somme: Pour un usage analytique de la scolastique médiévale (In total: For an analytical usage of medieval scholarship). Lagrasse:* Verdier, 2011.

Braudel, Fernand. *The Mediterranean and the Mediterranean World in the Age of Philip II of Spain.* Translated by Sîan Reynolds. New York: Harper & Row, 1972.

———»Personal Testimony.» *Journal of Modern History* 44 (1972): 448–67.

Breisach, Ernst A. *American Progressive History: An Experiment in Modernization.* Chicago, IL: Chicago University Press, 1993.

Burgière, André. *The Annales School: An Intellectual History.* Translated from the French by Jane Marie Todd. Ithaca, NY: Cornell University Press, 2009.

Burke, Peter. "The *Annales* in Global Context." *International Review of Social History* 35 (1990): 421–32.

———. *The French Historical Revolution: The Annales School, 1929–1989.* Stanford, CA: Stanford University Press, 1990.

Burrow, John. *A History of Histories: Epics, Chronicles, Romances & Inquiries from Herodotus and Thucydides to the Twentieth Century.* London: Allen Lane, 2007.

Busson, Henri. *Les Sources et le développement du rationalisme dans la littérature française de la Rénaissance, 1533–1601* (The sources and development of rationalism in the French literature of the Renaissance, 1533–1601). Paris: Letouzey, 1925.

Campbell, Peter R. "The New History: The *Annales* School of History and Modern Historiography." In *Historians and Historical Controversy*, edited by William Lamont, 5–22. London: UCL Press, 1999.

Carbonell, Charles-Olivier and Georges Livet, eds. *Au Berceau des Annales: Le Milieu strasbourgeois, l'histoire en France au début du XXe siècle* (At the crib of the *Annales*: The Strasbourg milieu, history in France at the beginning of the twentieth century). Toulouse: Presses de l'Institut d'Études Politiques de Toulouse, 1979.

Cavaillé, Jean-Pierre. «Les Frontières de l'inacceptable: Pour un réexamen de l'histoire de l'incrédulité» (The frontiers of the unacceptable: Toward a re-examination of the history of unbelief). *Les Dossiers du Grihl. Accessed October 20, 2014.* http://dossiersgrihl.revues.org/4746; doi: 10.4000/dossiersgrihl.4746

Chartier, Roger. *Lectures et lecteurs dans la France d'Ancien Régime.* Paris: Seuil, 1987.

Citron, Suzanne. «Positivisme, corporatisme et pouvoir dans la Société des professeurs d'histoire de 1910 à 1947» (Positivism, corporativism and power in the Society of History Professors from 1910 to 1947). *Revue Française de Science Politique* 27 (1977): 691–716.

Clark, Stuart, ed. *The Annales School: Critical Assessments.* 4 vols. London: Routledge, 1999.

Conrad, Sebastian. "Enlightenment in Global History: A Historiographical Critique." *American Historical Review* 117 (2012): 999—1027.

———. *The Quest for the Lost Nation: Writing History in America and Japan in the American Century.* Translated by Alan Nothnagle. Berkeley: University of

California Press, 2010.

Darnton, Robert. *L'Aventure de l'Encyclopédie.* Cambridge, MA: Harvard University Press, 1979.

————. *The Great Cat Massacre and Other Episodes in French Cultural History.* New York: Basic, 1984.

Davis, Natalie Zemon. "Beyond Babel: Multiple Tongues and National Identities in Rabelais and his Critics." In *Confronting the Turkish Dogs: A Conversation on Rabelais and His Critics*, edited by Timothy Hampton, 15–28. Berkeley: University of California Press, 1998.

Davis, Natalie Zemon and Denis Crouzet. *A Passion for History. Natalie Zemon David, Conversation with Denis Crouzet.* Kirksville, MO: Truman State University Press, 2010.

Denonain, Jean-Jacques. "Le Livre des trois imposteurs" (The book of three imposters). In *Aspects du libertinisme au XVIᵉ siècle* (Aspects of sixteenth-century libertinism), edited by Marcel Bataillon, 215–26. Paris: Albin Michel,1974.

Dewald, Jonathon. *Lost Worlds: The Emergence of French Social History 1815–1970.* Pennsylvania PA: Pennsylvania State University Press, 2006.

————. "Lost Worlds: French Historians and the Construction of Modernity." *French History* 14 (2000): 424–42.

Dosse, François. *Empire of Meaning: The Humanization of the Human Sciences.* Translated by Hassan Melehy, 229–30. Minneapolis: Minnesota University Press, 1999.

————. *L'Histoire en miettes: Des "Annales" à la "nouvelle histoire"* (History in pieces: From the "*Annales*" to the "new history"). Paris: Seuil, 1987.

Durkheim, Émile. *Les Règles de la méthode sociologique* (The rules of the sociological method). Paris: Alcan, 1895.

Duvignaud, Jean. "Review of Lucien Febvre, *Le Problème de l'incroyance au XVIᵉ siècle. La Religion de Rabelais.*" *L'Année Sociologique* 1 (1940): 454.

Evennett, H. O. "Review of Lucien Febvre, *Au Coeur réligieux du XVIᵉ siècle.*" *English Historical Review* 73 (1958): 523.

Febvre, Lucien. *Combats pour l'histoire* (Combats for history). Paris: Armand Colin, 1952.

————. «Histoire des idées, histoire des sociétés: Une Question de climat» (History of ideas, history of societies: A question of climate). *Annales. Histoire, Sciences Sociales* 2 (1946): 158–61.

— — —. «L'Homme, la légende et l'œuvre. Sur Rabelais: Ignorances fondamentales.» *Revue de Synthèse* 1 (1931): 1–31.

— — —. *Martin Luther: Un Destin* (Martin Luther: A destiny). Paris: Presses Universitaires de France, 1928.

— — —. *Origène et Des Périers, ou l'énigme du* Cymbalum Mundi. Paris: Droz, 1942.

— — —. «Une Question mal posée: Les Origines de la Réforme française et le problème général des causes de la Réforme» (An ill-conceived question: The origins of the French Reformation and the general problem of the causes of the Reformation). *Revue Historique* 161 (1929): 1–73.

— — —. «Review of Henri Jassemin, *Le Chambre des Comptes de Paris*» (The Chamber of Accounts of Paris). *Annales d'Histoire Économique et Sociale* 6 (1934): 148–53.

— — —. «Sur Einstein et sur l'histoire: Méditation de circonstance» (On Einstein and history: A meditation on circumstances). *Annales. Économies, Sociétés, Civilisations* 10 (1955): 305–12.

— — —. «Vers une autre histoire» (Toward another history). *Revue de Métaphysique et de Morale* 63 (1949): 233, 229.

— — —. «Aux Origines de l'esprit moderne: Libertinisme, naturalisme, mécanisme» (On the origins of the modern spirit: Libertinism, naturalism and mechanism). In *Au Cœur religieux du XVIᵉ siècle*, Lucien Febvre, 337–58. Paris: Editions EHESS, 1957.

— — —. «Dolet, Propagator of the Gospel» (1945). In Lucien Febvre, *A New Kind of History*, edited by Peter Burke, 108–59. London: Harper & Row, 1973.

— — —. *The Problem of Unbelief in the Sixteenth Century: The Religion of Rabelais*, translated by Beatrice Gottlieb. Cambridge, MA: Harvard University Press, 1982.

Febvre, Lucien and Henri-Jean Martin. *L'Apparition du livre*. Paris: Albin Michel, 1957.

France, Anatole. *Rabelais.* Paris: Calmann-Lévy, 1928.

Gemelli, Giuliana. *Fernand Braudel.* Translated into French by Brigitte Pasquet and Béatrice Propetto Marzi. Paris: Odile Jacob, 1995.

Gilson, Étienne. *Les Idées et les lettres: Essais d'Art et de Philosophie* (Ideas and literature: Essays on art and philosophy). Paris: Vrin, 1932.

Ginzburg, Carlo. *The Cheese and the Worms: The Cosmos of a Sixteenth-Century Miller*. Baltimore, MD: Johns Hopkins University Press, 1980.

Grafton, Anthony. *Cardano's Cosmos: The Worlds and Works of a Renaissance Astrologer.* Cambridge, MA: Harvard University Press, 2001.

Guldi, Jo and David Armitage. *The History Manifesto*. Cambridge: Cambridge University Press, 2014.

Harris, Ruth. *The Man on Devil's Island: Alfred Dreyfus and the Affair that Divided France*. London: Allen Lane, 2005.

Hauser, Henri. «De l'humanisme et de la Reforme en France.» *Revue Historique* 64 (*1897*): 258–9.

Hill, Christopher. "Irreligion in the Puritan Revolution." In *Radical Religion in the English Revolution*, edited by J. F. McGregor and Barry Reay, 191–211. Oxford: Oxford University Press, 1984.

Hughes-Warrington, Marnie. *Fifty Key Thinkers on History.* London: Routledge, 2000.

Hunt, Lynn. "French History in the Last Twenty Years: The Rise and Fall of the Annales Paradigm." *The Journal of Contemporary History* 21 (1986), 209–24.

Hyslop, Beatrice F. "Review of Bloch, *Apologie pour l'histoire*" (Apology for history). *American Historical Review* 55 (1950): 866–8.

Iggers Georg G. and Edward Wang. *A Global History of Modern Historiography.* London: Routledge, 2008.

Kastler, Jean-Loup. «Du 'problème de l'incroyance' à 'l'étrange liberté': Un changement de paradigme de l'histoire des expériences religieuses?» (From "the problem of unbelief" to "the strange liberty": A change of paradigm in the history of religious experiences?). *Théorèmes* 5 (2013): 63–82.

Kedward, Rod. *La Vie en bleu: France and the French since 1900.* London: Allen Lane, 2005.

Kocka, Jürgen. "Comparison and Beyond." *History and Theory* 42 (2003): 39–44.

Langlois, Charles-Victor. *La Vie en France au Moyen Âge d'après quelques moralistes du temps* (Life in medieval France according to some moralists of the period). Paris; Hachette, 1908.

Le Bars, Stéphane. «Les Revendications identitaires sont inquiétantes: Le Président de l'Observatoire de la laïcité défend une conception du combat laïque qui va au-delà de la loi de 1905» (Claims about identity cause concern: The president of the Secular Observatory defends an illegal vision of secular combat that continues outside of the law of 1905). *Le Monde*, July 4, 2010, 8.

Lefranc, Abel. *Les Navigations de Pantagruel* (The seafaring of Pantagruel). Paris: Leclerc, 1905.

Le Goff, Jacques. "Is Politics Still the Backbone of History?" *Daedalus: Journal of the American Academy of Arts and Sciences* 100 (1971): 1–19.

— — —. *La Naissance du Purgatoire* (The birth of purgatory). Translated by Arthur Goldhammer. Aldershot: Scolar Press, 1990.

Lenoble, Robert. *Mersenne, ou la naissance du mécanisme.* Paris: Vrin, 1943.

Le Roy Ladurie, Emmanuel. *Montaillou: Village Occitain de 1294 à 1324* (Montaillou: Languedoc village from 1294 until 1324). Paris: Gallimard, 1975.

— — —. *Les Paysans de Languedoc* (The peasants of Languedoc, 2 vols.). Paris: SEVPEN, 1966.

Lévy-Bruhl, Lucien. *La Mentalité primitive.* Paris: PUF, 1922.

Lovejoy, Arthur O. *The Great Chain of Being.* Cambridge, MA: Harvard University Press, 1936.

Michelet, Jules. *Le Peuple: Nos fils* (The people: Our sons). Paris: Flammarion, 1846.

Monod, Gabriel. *Renan, Taine, Michelet: Les Maîtres d'histoire* (Renan, Taine, Michelet: The masters of history). Paris: Calmann-Lévy, 1894.

Müller, Bertrand, ed. *Marc Bloch, Lucien Febvre et les Annales d'Histoire économique et sociale: Correspondance*, Bloch to Febvre, June 18, 1938. Paris: Fayard, 1994–2003.

— — —. *Lucien Febvre: Lecteur et critique* (Lucien Febvre: Reader and critic). Paris: Albin Michel, 1994.

Nora, Pierre, *Les Lieux de mémoire* (Places of memory). Paris: Gallimard, 1997.

Noronha-DiVanna, Isabel. *Writing History in the Third Republic.* Newcastle upon Tyne: Cambridge Scholars Publishing, 2010.

O'Malley, John W. *Trent and All That: Renaming Catholicism in the Early-Modern Era.* Cambridge, MA: Harvard University Press, 2002.

Partner, Nancy and Sarah Foot, eds. *The Sage Handbook of Historical Theory.* London: Sage, 2013.

Picquier, Marcel. *Étienne Dolet (1509—1546): Imprimeur humaniste lyonnais mort sur le bûcher* (Étienne Dolet (1509—1546): Humanist printer of Lyons dead on the pyre). Lyons: Association laïque lyonnaise des Amis d'Étienne Dolet, 2009.

Pintard, René. *Le Libertinage érudit.* Paris: Boivin, 1943.

Pluet-Despatin, Jacqueline and Giles Candar, eds. *Lucien Febvre: Lettres à*

Henri Berr. Paris: Fayard, 1997.

Rebérioux, Madeleine. «Histoire, historiens et dreyfusisme» (History, historians and support for Dreyfus). *Revue Historique* 518 (1976): 407–9.

Ricoeur, Paul. *The Contribution of French Historiography to the Theory of History: The Zaharoff Lecture for 1978–1979.* Oxford: Clarendon Press, 1980.

———. *Memory, History, Forgetting.* Translated by Kathleen Blamey and David Pellauer. Chicago, IL: Chicago University Press, 2004.

Ringer, Fritz K. *The Decline of the German Mandarins: The German Academic Community 1890—1933.* Cambridge, MA: Harvard University Press, 1990.

Ross Sorkin, Andrew. "So Bill Gates Has This Idea for a History Class." *New York Times*, September 5, 2014. Accessed October 30, 2014. http://www.nytimes.com/2014/09/07/magazine/so-bill-gates-has-this-idea-for-a-history-class.html?_r=1.

Schöttler, Peter. «Le Rhin comme enjeu historiographique dans l'entre-deux-guerres. Vers une histoire des mentalités frontalières" (The Rhine as a historiographical stake in the inter-war period. Toward a history of frontier mentalities). *Genèses* 14 (1994): 63–82.

Simiand, François. «La Causalité en histoire» (Causation in history). *Bulletin de la Société Française de Philosophie* 6 (1906): 247–74.

———. «Méthode historique et science sociale: Étude critique d'après les ouvrages récents de M. Lacombe et de M. Seignobos» (Historical method and social science: A critical study in response to the recent works of Lacombe and Seignobos). *Revue de Synthèse Historique* 2 (1902): 1–22; 128–77.

———. *La Méthode positive en science économique* (Positive method and economic science). Paris: Alcan, 1912.

Spencer, Nick. *Atheists: The Origin of the Species.* London: Bloomsbury, 2014.

Stoianovich, Traian. *French Historical Method: The Annales Paradigm.* Ithaca, NY: Cornell University Press, 1976.

Taylor, A. J. P. Review of Renouvin, *Histoire des Relations Internationales* (History of international relations). *English Historical Review* 70 (1955): 503–4.

Tendler, Joseph. "*Annales* Historians' Contested Transformations of Locality." In *Place and Locality in Modern France*, edited by Philip Whalen and Patrick Hutton, 53–64. London: Bloomsbury, 2014.

———.*Opponents of the Annales School.* Basingstoke: Palgrave, 2013.

———. "Variations on Realism, Method and Time: The *Annales* School." In *The Sage Handbook of Historical Theory*, edited by Nancy Partner and Sarah

Foot, 67–80. London: Sage, 2013.

Thuasne, Louis. *Études sur Rabelais* (Studies of Rabelais). Paris: Bouillon, 1904.

Veysey, Laurence R. *The Emergence of the American University*. Chicago, IL: Chicago University Press, 1965.

Weber, Eugen. *The Hollow Years: France in the 1930s.* New York: Norton, 1996.

Weber, Max. *The Protestant Ethic and the Spirit of Capitalism.* Translated by Talcott Parsons. New York: Scribner, 1930.

Wirth, Jean. *Croyants et sceptiques au XVIᵉ siècle: Le Dossier des Epicuriens* (Believers and skeptics in the sixteenth century: The Epicurean file). Strasbourg: Strasbourg University Press, 1981.

———. "'Libertins' et 'Epicuriens': Aspects de l'irréligion au XVIᵉ siècle," ("Libertines" and "Epicureans": Aspects of irreligion in the sixteenth century). *Bibliothèque d'Humanisme et Renaissance* 29 (1977): 601–27.

Wootton, David. "Lucien Febvre and the Problem of Unbelief in the Early Modern Period." *Journal of Modern History* 60 (1988): 695–730.

THE MACAT LIBRARY
BY DISCIPLINE

AFRICANA STUDIES

Chinua Achebe's *An Image of Africa: Racism in Conrad's Heart of Darkness*
W. E. B. Du Bois's *The Souls of Black Folk*
Zora Neale Huston's *Characteristics of Negro Expression*
Martin Luther King Jr's *Why We Can't Wait*
Toni Morrison's *Playing in the Dark: Whiteness in the American Literary Imagination*

ANTHROPOLOGY

Arjun Appadurai's *Modernity at Large: Cultural Dimensions of Globalisation*
Philippe Ariès's *Centuries of Childhood*
Franz Boas's *Race, Language and Culture*
Kim Chan & Renée Mauborgne's *Blue Ocean Strategy*
Jared Diamond's *Guns, Germs & Steel: the Fate of Human Societies*
Jared Diamond's *Collapse: How Societies Choose to Fail or Survive*
E. E. Evans-Pritchard's *Witchcraft, Oracles and Magic Among the Azande*
James Ferguson's *The Anti-Politics Machine*
Clifford Geertz's *The Interpretation of Cultures*
David Graeber's *Debt: the First 5000 Years*
Karen Ho's *Liquidated: An Ethnography of Wall Street*
Geert Hofstede's *Culture's Consequences: Comparing Values, Behaviors, Institutes and Organizations across Nations*
Claude Lévi-Strauss's *Structural Anthropology*
Jay Macleod's *Ain't No Makin' It: Aspirations and Attainment in a Low-Income Neighborhood*
Saba Mahmood's *The Politics of Piety: The Islamic Revival and the Feminist Subjec*t
Marcel Mauss's *The Gift*

BUSINESS

Jean Lave & Etienne Wenger's *Situated Learning*
Theodore Levitt's *Marketing Myopia*
Burton G. Malkiel's *A Random Walk Down Wall Street*
Douglas McGregor's *The Human Side of Enterprise*
Michael Porter's *Competitive Strategy: Creating and Sustaining Superior Performance*
John Kotter's *Leading Change*
C. K. Prahalad & Gary Hamel's *The Core Competence of the Corporation*

CRIMINOLOGY

Michelle Alexander's *The New Jim Crow: Mass Incarceration in the Age of Colorblindness*
Michael R. Gottfredson & Travis Hirschi's *A General Theory of Crime*
Richard Herrnstein & Charles A. Murray's *The Bell Curve: Intelligence and Class Structure in American Life*
Elizabeth Loftus's *Eyewitness Testimony*
Jay Macleod's *Ain't No Makin' It: Aspirations and Attainment in a Low-Income Neighborhood*
Philip Zimbardo's *The Lucifer Effect*

ECONOMICS

Janet Abu-Lughod's *Before European Hegemony*
Ha-Joon Chang's *Kicking Away the Ladder*
David Brion Davis's *The Problem of Slavery in the Age of Revolution*
Milton Friedman's *The Role of Monetary Policy*
Milton Friedman's *Capitalism and Freedom*
David Graeber's *Debt: the First 5000 Years*
Friedrich Hayek's *The Road to Serfdom*
Karen Ho's *Liquidated: An Ethnography of Wall Street*

The Macat Library By Discipline

John Maynard Keynes's *The General Theory of Employment, Interest and Money*
Charles P. Kindleberger's *Manias, Panics and Crashes*
Robert Lucas's *Why Doesn't Capital Flow from Rich to Poor Countries?*
Burton G. Malkiel's *A Random Walk Down Wall Street*
Thomas Robert Malthus's *An Essay on the Principle of Population*
Karl Marx's *Capital*
Thomas Piketty's *Capital in the Twenty-First Century*
Amartya Sen's *Development as Freedom*
Adam Smith's *The Wealth of Nations*
Nassim Nicholas Taleb's *The Black Swan: The Impact of the Highly Improbable*
Amos Tversky's & Daniel Kahneman's *Judgment under Uncertainty: Heuristics and Biases*
Mahbub Ul Haq's *Reflections on Human Development*
Max Weber's *The Protestant Ethic and the Spirit of Capitalism*

FEMINISM AND GENDER STUDIES

Judith Butler's *Gender Trouble*
Simone De Beauvoir's *The Second Sex*
Michel Foucault's *History of Sexuality*
Betty Friedan's *The Feminine Mystique*
Saba Mahmood's *The Politics of Piety: The Islamic Revival and the Feminist Subject*
Joan Wallach Scott's *Gender and the Politics of History*
Mary Wollstonecraft's *A Vindication of the Rights of Woman*
Virginia Woolf's *A Room of One's Own*

GEOGRAPHY

The Brundtland Report's *Our Common Future*
Rachel Carson's *Silent Spring*
Charles Darwin's *On the Origin of Species*
James Ferguson's *The Anti-Politics Machine*
Jane Jacobs's *The Death and Life of Great American Cities*
James Lovelock's *Gaia: A New Look at Life on Earth*
Amartya Sen's *Development as Freedom*
Mathis Wackernagel & William Rees's *Our Ecological Footprint*

HISTORY

Janet Abu-Lughod's *Before European Hegemony*
Benedict Anderson's *Imagined Communities*
Bernard Bailyn's *The Ideological Origins of the American Revolution*
Hanna Batatu's *The Old Social Classes And The Revolutionary Movements Of Iraq*
Christopher Browning's *Ordinary Men: Reserve Police Batallion 101 and the Final Solution in Poland*
Edmund Burke's *Reflections on the Revolution in France*
William Cronon's *Nature's Metropolis: Chicago And The Great West*
Alfred W. Crosby's *The Columbian Exchange*
Hamid Dabashi's *Iran: A People Interrupted*
David Brion Davis's *The Problem of Slavery in the Age of Revolution*
Nathalie Zemon Davis's *The Return of Martin Guerre*
Jared Diamond's *Guns, Germs & Steel: the Fate of Human Societies*
Frank Dikotter's *Mao's Great Famine*
John W Dower's *War Without Mercy: Race And Power In The Pacific War*
W. E. B. Du Bois's *The Souls of Black Folk*
Richard J. Evans's *In Defence of History*
Lucien Febvre's *The Problem of Unbelief in the 16th Century*
Sheila Fitzpatrick's *Everyday Stalinism*

Eric Foner's *Reconstruction: America's Unfinished Revolution, 1863-1877*
Michel Foucault's *Discipline and Punish*
Michel Foucault's *History of Sexuality*
Francis Fukuyama's *The End of History and the Last Man*
John Lewis Gaddis's *We Now Know: Rethinking Cold War History*
Ernest Gellner's *Nations and Nationalism*
Eugene Genovese's *Roll, Jordan, Roll: The World the Slaves Made*
Carlo Ginzburg's *The Night Battles*
Daniel Goldhagen's *Hitler's Willing Executioners*
Jack Goldstone's *Revolution and Rebellion in the Early Modern World*
Antonio Gramsci's *The Prison Notebooks*
Alexander Hamilton, John Jay & James Madison's *The Federalist Papers*
Christopher Hill's *The World Turned Upside Down*
Carole Hillenbrand's *The Crusades: Islamic Perspectives*
Thomas Hobbes's *Leviathan*
Eric Hobsbawm's *The Age Of Revolution*
John A. Hobson's *Imperialism: A Study*
Albert Hourani's *History of the Arab Peoples*
Samuel P. Huntington's *The Clash of Civilizations and the Remaking of World Order*
C. L. R. James's *The Black Jacobins*
Tony Judt's *Postwar: A History of Europe Since 1945*
Ernst Kantorowicz's *The King's Two Bodies: A Study in Medieval Political Theology*
Paul Kennedy's *The Rise and Fall of the Great Powers*
Ian Kershaw's *The "Hitler Myth": Image and Reality in the Third Reich*
John Maynard Keynes's *The General Theory of Employment, Interest and Money*
Charles P. Kindleberger's *Manias, Panics and Crashes*
Martin Luther King Jr's *Why We Can't Wait*
Henry Kissinger's *World Order: Reflections on the Character of Nations and the Course of History*
Thomas Kuhn's *The Structure of Scientific Revolutions*
Georges Lefebvre's *The Coming of the French Revolution*
John Locke's *Two Treatises of Government*
Niccolò Machiavelli's *The Prince*
Thomas Robert Malthus's *An Essay on the Principle of Population*
Mahmood Mamdani's *Citizen and Subject: Contemporary Africa And The Legacy Of Late Colonialism*
Karl Marx's *Capital*
Stanley Milgram's *Obedience to Authority*
John Stuart Mill's *On Liberty*
Thomas Paine's *Common Sense*
Thomas Paine's *Rights of Man*
Geoffrey Parker's *Global Crisis: War, Climate Change and Catastrophe in the Seventeenth Century*
Jonathan Riley-Smith's *The First Crusade and the Idea of Crusading*
Jean-Jacques Rousseau's *The Social Contract*
Joan Wallach Scott's *Gender and the Politics of History*
Theda Skocpol's *States and Social Revolutions*
Adam Smith's *The Wealth of Nations*
Timothy Snyder's *Bloodlands: Europe Between Hitler and Stalin*
Sun Tzu's *The Art of War*
Keith Thomas's *Religion and the Decline of Magic*
Thucydides's *The History of the Peloponnesian War*
Frederick Jackson Turner's *The Significance of the Frontier in American History*
Odd Arne Westad's *The Global Cold War: Third World Interventions And The Making Of Our Times*

LITERATURE

Chinua Achebe's *An Image of Africa: Racism in Conrad's Heart of Darkness*
Roland Barthes's *Mythologies*
Homi K. Bhabha's *The Location of Culture*
Judith Butler's *Gender Trouble*
Simone De Beauvoir's *The Second Sex*
Ferdinand De Saussure's *Course in General Linguistics*
T. S. Eliot's *The Sacred Wood: Essays on Poetry and Criticism*
Zora Neale Huston's *Characteristics of Negro Expression*
Toni Morrison's *Playing in the Dark: Whiteness in the American Literary Imagination*
Edward Said's *Orientalism*
Gayatri Chakravorty Spivak's *Can the Subaltern Speak?*
Mary Wollstonecraft's *A Vindication of the Rights of Women*
Virginia Woolf's *A Room of One's Own*

PHILOSOPHY

Elizabeth Anscombe's *Modern Moral Philosophy*
Hannah Arendt's *The Human Condition*
Aristotle's *Metaphysics*
Aristotle's *Nicomachean Ethics*
Edmund Gettier's *Is Justified True Belief Knowledge?*
Georg Wilhelm Friedrich Hegel's *Phenomenology of Spirit*
David Hume's *Dialogues Concerning Natural Religion*
David Hume's *The Enquiry for Human Understanding*
Immanuel Kant's *Religion within the Boundaries of Mere Reason*
Immanuel Kant's *Critique of Pure Reason*
Søren Kierkegaard's *The Sickness Unto Death*
Søren Kierkegaard's *Fear and Trembling*
C. S. Lewis's *The Abolition of Man*
Alasdair MacIntyre's *After Virtue*
Marcus Aurelius's *Meditations*
Friedrich Nietzsche's *On the Genealogy of Morality*
Friedrich Nietzsche's *Beyond Good and Evil*
Plato's *Republic*
Plato's *Symposium*
Jean-Jacques Rousseau's *The Social Contract*
Gilbert Ryle's *The Concept of Mind*
Baruch Spinoza's *Ethics*
Sun Tzu's *The Art of War*
Ludwig Wittgenstein's *Philosophical Investigations*

POLITICS

Benedict Anderson's *Imagined Communities*
Aristotle's *Politics*
Bernard Bailyn's *The Ideological Origins of the American Revolution*
Edmund Burke's *Reflections on the Revolution in France*
John C. Calhoun's *A Disquisition on Government*
Ha-Joon Chang's *Kicking Away the Ladder*
Hamid Dabashi's *Iran: A People Interrupted*
Hamid Dabashi's *Theology of Discontent: The Ideological Foundation of the Islamic Revolution in Iran*
Robert Dahl's *Democracy and its Critics*
Robert Dahl's *Who Governs?*
David Brion Davis's *The Problem of Slavery in the Age of Revolution*

Alexis De Tocqueville's *Democracy in America*
James Ferguson's *The Anti-Politics Machine*
Frank Dikotter's *Mao's Great Famine*
Sheila Fitzpatrick's *Everyday Stalinism*
Eric Foner's *Reconstruction: America's Unfinished Revolution, 1863-1877*
Milton Friedman's *Capitalism and Freedom*
Francis Fukuyama's *The End of History and the Last Man*
John Lewis Gaddis's *We Now Know: Rethinking Cold War History*
Ernest Gellner's *Nations and Nationalism*
David Graeber's *Debt: the First 5000 Years*
Antonio Gramsci's *The Prison Notebooks*
Alexander Hamilton, John Jay & James Madison's *The Federalist Papers*
Friedrich Hayek's *The Road to Serfdom*
Christopher Hill's *The World Turned Upside Down*
Thomas Hobbes's *Leviathan*
John A. Hobson's *Imperialism: A Study*
Samuel P. Huntington's *The Clash of Civilizations and the Remaking of World Order*
Tony Judt's *Postwar: A History of Europe Since 1945*
David C. Kang's *China Rising: Peace, Power and Order in East Asia*
Paul Kennedy's *The Rise and Fall of Great Powers*
Robert Keohane's *After Hegemony*
Martin Luther King Jr.'s *Why We Can't Wait*
Henry Kissinger's *World Order: Reflections on the Character of Nations and the Course of History*
John Locke's *Two Treatises of Government*
Niccolò Machiavelli's *The Prince*
Thomas Robert Malthus's *An Essay on the Principle of Population*
Mahmood Mamdani's *Citizen and Subject: Contemporary Africa And The Legacy Of Late Colonialism*
Karl Marx's *Capital*
John Stuart Mill's *On Liberty*
John Stuart Mill's *Utilitarianism*
Hans Morgenthau's *Politics Among Nations*
Thomas Paine's *Common Sense*
Thomas Paine's *Rights of Man*
Thomas Piketty's *Capital in the Twenty-First Century*
Robert D. Putman's *Bowling Alone*
John Rawls's *Theory of Justice*
Jean-Jacques Rousseau's *The Social Contract*
Theda Skocpol's *States and Social Revolutions*
Adam Smith's *The Wealth of Nations*
Sun Tzu's *The Art of War*
Henry David Thoreau's *Civil Disobedience*
Thucydides's *The History of the Peloponnesian War*
Kenneth Waltz's *Theory of International Politics*
Max Weber's *Politics as a Vocation*
Odd Arne Westad's *The Global Cold War: Third World Interventions And The Making Of Our Times*

POSTCOLONIAL STUDIES

Roland Barthes's *Mythologies*
Frantz Fanon's *Black Skin, White Masks*
Homi K. Bhabha's *The Location of Culture*
Gustavo Gutiérrez's *A Theology of Liberation*
Edward Said's *Orientalism*
Gayatri Chakravorty Spivak's *Can the Subaltern Speak?*

The Macat Library By Discipline

PSYCHOLOGY

Gordon Allport's *The Nature of Prejudice*
Alan Baddeley & Graham Hitch's *Aggression: A Social Learning Analysis*
Albert Bandura's *Aggression: A Social Learning Analysis*
Leon Festinger's *A Theory of Cognitive Dissonance*
Sigmund Freud's *The Interpretation of Dreams*
Betty Friedan's *The Feminine Mystique*
Michael R. Gottfredson & Travis Hirschi's *A General Theory of Crime*
Eric Hoffer's *The True Believer: Thoughts on the Nature of Mass Movements*
William James's *Principles of Psychology*
Elizabeth Loftus's *Eyewitness Testimony*
A. H. Maslow's *A Theory of Human Motivation*
Stanley Milgram's *Obedience to Authority*
Steven Pinker's *The Better Angels of Our Nature*
Oliver Sacks's *The Man Who Mistook His Wife For a Hat*
Richard Thaler & Cass Sunstein's *Nudge: Improving Decisions About Health, Wealth and Happiness*
Amos Tversky's *Judgment under Uncertainty: Heuristics and Biases*
Philip Zimbardo's *The Lucifer Effect*

SCIENCE

Rachel Carson's *Silent Spring*
William Cronon's *Nature's Metropolis: Chicago And The Great West*
Alfred W. Crosby's *The Columbian Exchange*
Charles Darwin's *On the Origin of Species*
Richard Dawkin's *The Selfish Gene*
Thomas Kuhn's *The Structure of Scientific Revolutions*
Geoffrey Parker's *Global Crisis: War, Climate Change and Catastrophe in the Seventeenth Century*
Mathis Wackernagel & William Rees's *Our Ecological Footprint*

SOCIOLOGY

Michelle Alexander's *The New Jim Crow: Mass Incarceration in the Age of Colorblindness*
Gordon Allport's *The Nature of Prejudice*
Albert Bandura's *Aggression: A Social Learning Analysis*
Hanna Batatu's *The Old Social Classes And The Revolutionary Movements Of Iraq*
Ha-Joon Chang's *Kicking Away the Ladder*
W. E. B. Du Bois's *The Souls of Black Folk*
Émile Durkheim's *On Suicide*
Frantz Fanon's *Black Skin, White Masks*
Frantz Fanon's *The Wretched of the Earth*
Eric Foner's *Reconstruction: America's Unfinished Revolution, 1863-1877*
Eugene Genovese's *Roll, Jordan, Roll: The World the Slaves Made*
Jack Goldstone's *Revolution and Rebellion in the Early Modern World*
Antonio Gramsci's *The Prison Notebooks*
Richard Herrnstein & Charles A Murray's *The Bell Curve: Intelligence and Class Structure in American Life*
Eric Hoffer's *The True Believer: Thoughts on the Nature of Mass Movements*
Jane Jacobs's *The Death and Life of Great American Cities*
Robert Lucas's *Why Doesn't Capital Flow from Rich to Poor Countries?*
Jay Macleod's *Ain't No Makin' It: Aspirations and Attainment in a Low Income Neighborhood*
Elaine May's *Homeward Bound: American Families in the Cold War Era*
Douglas McGregor's *The Human Side of Enterprise*
C. Wright Mills's *The Sociological Imagination*

Thomas Piketty's *Capital in the Twenty-First Century*
Robert D. Putman's *Bowling Alone*
David Riesman's *The Lonely Crowd: A Study of the Changing American Character*
Edward Said's *Orientalism*
Joan Wallach Scott's *Gender and the Politics of History*
Theda Skocpol's *States and Social Revolutions*
Max Weber's *The Protestant Ethic and the Spirit of Capitalism*

THEOLOGY

Augustine's *Confessions*
Benedict's *Rule of St Benedict*
Gustavo Gutiérrez's *A Theology of Liberation*
Carole Hillenbrand's *The Crusades: Islamic Perspectives*
David Hume's *Dialogues Concerning Natural Religion*
Immanuel Kant's *Religion within the Boundaries of Mere Reason*
Ernst Kantorowicz's *The King's Two Bodies: A Study in Medieval Political Theology*
Søren Kierkegaard's *The Sickness Unto Death*
C. S. Lewis's *The Abolition of Man*
Saba Mahmood's *The Politics of Piety: The Islamic Revival and the Feminist Subject*
Baruch Spinoza's *Ethics*
Keith Thomas's *Religion and the Decline of Magic*

COMING SOON

Chris Argyris's *The Individual and the Organisation*
Seyla Benhabib's *The Rights of Others*
Walter Benjamin's *The Work Of Art in the Age of Mechanical Reproduction*
John Berger's *Ways of Seeing*
Pierre Bourdieu's *Outline of a Theory of Practice*
Mary Douglas's *Purity and Danger*
Roland Dworkin's *Taking Rights Seriously*
James G. March's *Exploration and Exploitation in Organisational Learning*
Ikujiro Nonaka's *A Dynamic Theory of Organizational Knowledge Creation*
Griselda Pollock's *Vision and Difference*
Amartya Sen's *Inequality Re-Examined*
Susan Sontag's *On Photography*
Yasser Tabbaa's *The Transformation of Islamic Art*
Ludwig von Mises's *Theory of Money and Credit*

Macat Disciplines

Access the greatest ideas and thinkers across entire disciplines, including

Postcolonial Studies

Roland Barthes's *Mythologies*
Frantz Fanon's *Black Skin, White Masks*
Homi K. Bhabha's *The Location of Culture*
Gustavo Gutiérrez's *A Theology of Liberation*
Edward Said's *Orientalism*
Gayatri Chakravorty Spivak's *Can the Subaltern Speak?*

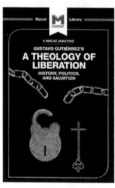
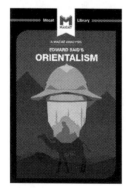

Macat analyses are available from all good bookshops and libraries.

Access hundreds of analyses through one, multimedia tool.
Join free for one month **library.macat.com**

Macat Disciplines

Access the greatest ideas and thinkers across entire disciplines, including

AFRICANA STUDIES

Chinua Achebe's *An Image of Africa: Racism in Conrad's Heart of Darkness*

W. E. B. Du Bois's *The Souls of Black Folk*

Zora Neale Hurston's *Characteristics of Negro Expression*

Martin Luther King Jr.'s *Why We Can't Wait*

Toni Morrison's *Playing in the Dark: Whiteness in the American Literary Imagination*

Macat analyses are available from all good bookshops and libraries.

Access hundreds of analyses through one, multimedia tool.
Join free for one month **library.macat.com**

Macat Disciplines

Access the greatest ideas and thinkers across entire disciplines, including

FEMINISM, GENDER AND QUEER STUDIES

Simone De Beauvoir's
The Second Sex

Michel Foucault's
History of Sexuality

Betty Friedan's
The Feminine Mystique

Saba Mahmood's
*The Politics of Piety:
The Islamic Revival and
the Feminist Subject*

Joan Wallach Scott's
*Gender and the
Politics of History*

Mary Wollstonecraft's
*A Vindication of the
Rights of Woman*

Virginia Woolf's
A Room of One's Own

Judith Butler's
Gender Trouble

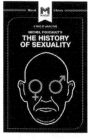

Macat analyses are available from all good bookshops and libraries.

Access hundreds of analyses through one, multimedia tool.
Join free for one month **library.macat.com**

Macat Disciplines

Access the greatest ideas and thinkers across entire disciplines, including

CRIMINOLOGY

Michelle Alexander's
The New Jim Crow: Mass Incarceration in the Age of Colorblindness

Michael R. Gottfredson & Travis Hirschi's
A General Theory of Crime

Elizabeth Loftus's
Eyewitness Testimony

Richard Herrnstein & Charles A. Murray's
The Bell Curve: Intelligence and Class Structure in American Life

Jay Macleod's
Ain't No Makin' It: Aspirations and Attainment in a Low-Income Neighborhood

Philip Zimbardo's
The Lucifer Effect

Macat Disciplines

Access the greatest ideas and thinkers across entire disciplines, including

INEQUALITY

Ha-Joon Chang's, *Kicking Away the Ladder*
David Graeber's, *Debt: The First 5000 Years*
Robert E. Lucas's, *Why Doesn't Capital Flow from Rich To Poor Countries?*
Thomas Piketty's, *Capital in the Twenty-First Century*
Amartya Sen's, *Inequality Re-Examined*
Mahbub Ul Haq's, *Reflections on Human Development*

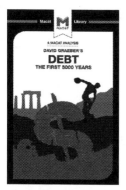

Macat analyses are available from all good bookshops and libraries.

Access hundreds of analyses through one, multimedia tool.
Join free for one month **library.macat.com**

Macat Disciplines

Access the greatest ideas and thinkers across entire disciplines, including

GLOBALIZATION

Arjun Appadurai's, *Modernity at Large: Cultural Dimensions of Globalisation*

James Ferguson's, *The Anti-Politics Machine*

Geert Hofstede's, *Culture's Consequences*

Amartya Sen's, *Development as Freedom*

Macat Disciplines

Access the greatest ideas and thinkers across entire disciplines, including

MAN AND THE ENVIRONMENT

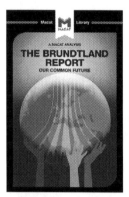

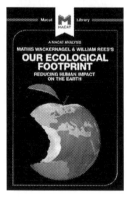

The Brundtland Report's, *Our Common Future*
Rachel Carson's, *Silent Spring*
James Lovelock's, *Gaia: A New Look at Life on Earth*
Mathis Wackernagel & William Rees's, *Our Ecological Footprint*

Macat Disciplines

Access the greatest ideas and thinkers across entire disciplines, including

THE FUTURE OF DEMOCRACY

Robert A. Dahl's, *Democracy and Its Critics*
Robert A. Dahl's, *Who Governs?*
Alexis De Toqueville's, *Democracy in America*
Niccolò Machiavelli's, *The Prince*
John Stuart Mill's, *On Liberty*
Robert D. Putnam's, *Bowling Alone*
Jean-Jacques Rousseau's, *The Social Contract*
Henry David Thoreau's, *Civil Disobedience*

Macat analyses are available from all good bookshops and libraries.

Access hundreds of analyses through one, multimedia tool.
Join free for one month **library.macat.com**

Macat Disciplines

Access the greatest ideas and thinkers across entire disciplines, including

TOTALITARIANISM

Sheila Fitzpatrick's, *Everyday Stalinism*
Ian Kershaw's, *The "Hitler Myth"*
Timothy Snyder's, *Bloodlands*

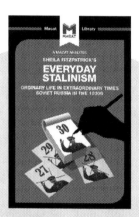

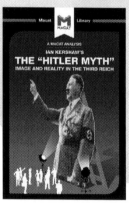

Macat Pairs

Analyse historical and modern issues from opposite sides of an argument. Pairs include:

RACE AND IDENTITY

Zora Neale Hurston's
Characteristics of Negro Expression

Using material collected on anthropological expeditions to the South, Zora Neale Hurston explains how expression in African American culture in the early twentieth century departs from the art of white America. At the time, African American art was often criticized for copying white culture. For Hurston, this criticism misunderstood how art works. European tradition views art as something fixed. But Hurston describes a creative process that is alive, ever-changing, and largely improvisational. She maintains that African American art works through a process called 'mimicry'—where an imitated object or verbal pattern, for example, is reshaped and altered until it becomes something new, novel—and worthy of attention.

Frantz Fanon's
Black Skin, White Masks

Black Skin, White Masks offers a radical analysis of the psychological effects of colonization on the colonized.

Fanon witnessed the effects of colonization first hand both in his birthplace, Martinique, and again later in life when he worked as a psychiatrist in another French colony, Algeria. His text is uncompromising in form and argument. He dissects the dehumanizing effects of colonialism, arguing that it destroys the native sense of identity, forcing people to adapt to an alien set of values—including a core belief that they are inferior. This results in deep psychological trauma.

Fanon's work played a pivotal role in the civil rights movements of the 1960s.

Macat Pairs

Analyse historical and modern issues from opposite sides of an argument. Pairs include:

INTERNATIONAL RELATIONS IN THE 21ST CENTURY

Samuel P. Huntington's
The Clash of Civilisations

In his highly influential 1996 book, Huntington offers a vision of a post-Cold War world in which conflict takes place not between competing ideologies but between cultures. The worst clash, he argues, will be between the Islamic world and the West: the West's arrogance and belief that its culture is a "gift" to the world will come into conflict with Islam's obstinacy and concern that its culture is under attack from a morally decadent "other."

Clash inspired much debate between different political schools of thought. But its greatest impact came in helping define American foreign policy in the wake of the 2001 terrorist attacks in New York and Washington.

Francis Fukuyama's
The End of History and the Last Man

Published in 1992, *The End of History and the Last Man* argues that capitalist democracy is the final destination for all societies. Fukuyama believed democracy triumphed during the Cold War because it lacks the "fundamental contradictions" inherent in communism and satisfies our yearning for freedom and equality. Democracy therefore marks the endpoint in the evolution of ideology, and so the "end of history." There will still be "events," but no fundamental change in ideology.

Macat Pairs

Analyse historical and modern issues from opposite sides of an argument. Pairs include:

HOW TO RUN AN ECONOMY

John Maynard Keynes's
The General Theory OF Employment, Interest and Money

Classical economics suggests that market economies are self-correcting in times of recession or depression, and tend toward full employment and output. But English economist John Maynard Keynes disagrees.

In his ground-breaking 1936 study *The General Theory*, Keynes argues that traditional economics has misunderstood the causes of unemployment. Employment is not determined by the price of labor; it is directly linked to demand. Keynes believes market economies are by nature unstable, and so require government intervention. Spurred on by the social catastrophe of the Great Depression of the 1930s, he sets out to revolutionize the way the world thinks

Milton Friedman's
The Role of Monetary Policy

Friedman's 1968 paper changed the course of economic theory. In just 17 pages, he demolished existing theory and outlined an effective alternate monetary policy designed to secure 'high employment, stable prices and rapid growth.'

Friedman demonstrated that monetary policy plays a vital role in broader economic stability and argued that economists got their monetary policy wrong in the 1950s and 1960s by misunderstanding the relationship between inflation and unemployment. Previous generations of economists had believed that governments could permanently decrease unemployment by permitting inflation—and vice versa. Friedman's most original contribution was to show that this supposed trade-off is an illusion that only works in the short term.

Macat analyses are available from all good bookshops and libraries.

Access hundreds of analyses through one, multimedia tool.
Join free for one month **library.macat.com**

Macat Pairs

Analyse historical and modern issues from opposite sides of an argument. Pairs include:

ARE WE FUNDAMENTALLY GOOD - OR BAD?

Steven Pinker's
The Better Angels of Our Nature

Stephen Pinker's gloriously optimistic 2011 book argues that, despite humanity's biological tendency toward violence, we are, in fact, less violent today than ever before. To prove his case, Pinker lays out pages of detailed statistical evidence. For him, much of the credit for the decline goes to the eighteenth-century Enlightenment movement, whose ideas of liberty, tolerance, and respect for the value of human life filtered down through society and affected how people thought. That psychological change led to behavioral change—and overall we became more peaceful. Critics countered that humanity could never overcome the biological urge toward violence; others argued that Pinker's statistics were flawed.

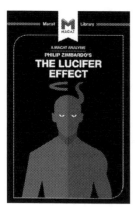

Philip Zimbardo's
The Lucifer Effect

Some psychologists believe those who commit cruelty are innately evil. Zimbardo disagrees. In *The Lucifer Effect*, he argues that sometimes good people do evil things simply because of the situations they find themselves in, citing many historical examples to illustrate his point. Zimbardo details his 1971 Stanford prison experiment, where ordinary volunteers playing guards in a mock prison rapidly became abusive. But he also describes the tortures committed by US army personnel in Iraq's Abu Ghraib prison in 2003—and how he himself testified in defence of one of those guards. committed by US army personnel in Iraq's Abu Ghraib prison in 2003—and how he himself testified in defence of one of those guards.

Macat analyses are available from all good bookshops and libraries.

Access hundreds of analyses through one, multimedia tool.
Join free for one month **library.macat.com**

Macat Pairs

Analyse historical and modern issues from opposite sides of an argument. Pairs include:

HOW WE RELATE TO EACH OTHER AND SOCIETY

Jean-Jacques Rousseau's
The Social Contract

Rousseau's famous work sets out the radical concept of the 'social contract': a give-and-take relationship between individual freedom and social order.

If people are free to do as they like, governed only by their own sense of justice, they are also vulnerable to chaos and violence. To avoid this, Rousseau proposes, they should agree to give up some freedom to benefit from the protection of social and political organization. But this deal is only just if societies are led by the collective needs and desires of the people, and able to control the private interests of individuals. For Rousseau, the only legitimate form of government is rule by the people.

Robert D. Putnam's
Bowling Alone

In *Bowling Alone*, Robert Putnam argues that Americans have become disconnected from one another and from the institutions of their common life, and investigates the consequences of this change.

Looking at a range of indicators, from membership in formal organizations to the number of invitations being extended to informal dinner parties, Putnam demonstrates that Americans are interacting less and creating less "social capital" – with potentially disastrous implications for their society.

It would be difficult to overstate the impact of *Bowling Alone*, one of the most frequently cited social science publications of the last half-century.

Macat analyses are available from all good bookshops and libraries.

Access hundreds of analyses through one, multimedia tool.
Join free for one month **library.macat.com**

Printed in the United States
by Baker & Taylor Publisher Services